Grief and the Spirit World

A Search for Comfort

by
Diane Kirby

◆ FriesenPress

One Printers Way
Altona, MB R0G 0B0
Canada

www.friesenpress.com

ISBN
978-1-03-916667-7 (Hardcover)
978-1-03-916666-0 (Paperback)
978-1-03-916668-4 (eBook)

1. BIOGRAPHY & AUTOBIOGRAPHY, PERSONAL MEMOIRS

Distributed to the trade by The Ingram Book Company

Dedicated to all who walk with me on this journey,
my ancestors, my soul mate David, and
the members of the Light Within—my tribe

Table of Contents

INTRODUCTION

People have always believed there is life after death. From ancient civilizations to indigenous people, all races have thought that some part of our being continues to live on in some form after the death of the physical body. It is why various cultures, such as Vikings and the ancient Egyptians, placed funerary objects (including food) in the graves of the deceased. Even the Neanderthal species did this a hundred thousand years ago, leading us to believe that they also thought that physical death was not the end of a journey.

Over the centuries, philosophers, writers, and scientists have all wrestled with the big questions about life, death, and the soul. There are no universally accepted conclusions in this regard. But it should come as no surprise to anyone that all religions embody these concepts, with the details of each being simply variations on a theme. Despite labels such as heaven, hell, the afterlife, the other side of the veil, and other monikers, the fact remains that approximately three-quarters of the North American population admits to believing in life after death.

Now, this is not to say that all of these people possess the same views. They do not. Beliefs regarding where souls go and why, or what happens after they get there, are as individual as the people holding them. And I take no position on any of them. The critical point is that most of us have accepted an expanded view of life and death, more akin to a continuum of life. It runs from a soul life to a physical/soul life to physical death to a return to a soul life.

In my case, this belief was introduced to me at an early age as fact. In my family, people spoke to those who had passed over, so the first step that life continued after death was a given. My family came from the Highlands of Scotland, where these beliefs are widely held. And as it happens in this region, a number of my family relations had varying degrees of two sights: regular sight and sight into the spirit world. More commonly referred to as second sight, these psychic abilities can pass down through blood-related family members. I was born with them. It seems I have had them all my life.

However, there is a difference between possessing these abilities and being able to use them. I never believed I had any gifts. Perhaps I thought this because they never intruded into my life. Or maybe I did not recognize them for what they were, if and when they did. I definitely never paid any attention to them, and I did not even think to explore them.

Then, my husband and life partner of forty-six years died, and I sank to the lowest point of my life. Lost in my grief, I turned back to my spiritual heritage to find some comfort for my pain and some peace for my soul. That is when I realized what kind of capabilities I had. I learned how to use them. I discovered that not only could I use my skills to heal myself, but I could also use them to heal others. And healing others healed me even more. Sometimes, we need to return to our roots, and embrace the core of who we are, to heal ourselves from hurt. I know this because it is what I did.

The heart may stop beating, but it never stops loving.
David Kirby

PROLOGUE

Dear David,

In the beginning, you were all in my heart. Swept up in the first rush of falling in love, life with you was a whirlwind of emotion, over-powering feelings, and the anticipation of what might come next. It took me quite a while before I could think straight when you were around.

In the middle, you still filled my heart, but my head came into play too. It had to. You were such a force, a whirling dervish of possibilities, ideas, and plans. You had an uncanny ability to recognize any opportunity and seize upon it, particularly if it meant having fun. And you were fearless, a quality I admired but could never acquire. (There was a reason you raced cars, and I cheered you on from the stands.) You worked hard, and you played harder, ensuring you experienced as much as possible before you left this earth. You wasted very few minutes of your life. I sometimes think you wore yourself out, for you were a handful from the get-go, but you were my handful, and I always had a firm, loving grip on you.

In the end, you are, once again, all in my heart. Overwhelmed by feelings of despair as I attempt to navigate this new relationship with you, my life has settled into a state I would generously describe as peaceful, something we rarely experienced together. Frankly, sweetie, I am not a fan. I miss your unrelenting energy, the constant movement throughout the house, and your never-ending cries of "Let's," "We should," and "Do you want to?" I miss you taking me with you to the edge—past the limits of my knowledge, to the first step of new experiences, and the jumping-off points to unknown adventures. The absence of your childlike wonder and enthusiasm beckoning me, amusing me, and enjoying new discoveries with me truly haunts me. It has been extremely hard going to acclimate to life in the vacuum-like void that now surrounds me, even though I need the silence to be able to hear you now.

Please forgive me if I shed a tear while adjusting to the pace of this new life, even though I know in my heart and my head that you and our love are with me always.

Forever loved,
Diane xo

1. IN THE BEGINNING

All mothers know things. There is even a name for it: mother's intuition. But my mother had a deeper knowing that transcended the normal range of such parental awareness. As time went on, I became aware that she seemed to have more direct knowledge of what was going on in my life compared to my friends and their mothers. And yet, I never questioned it. I never asked her how she learned things about my life that she should not have known. Her abilities were just accepted as a normal undercurrent in our home.

Then, one day, the undercurrent turned into a tidal wave I could not ignore. I stood in the shower replaying the events of the night before. As wonderful as the night had been, I had no intention of sharing any of the details of it with my parents. As various thoughts ran through my nineteen-year-old head, one thought in particular repeated itself several times. I finally abandoned the shower and completed the remaining steps of my morning routine. I arrived at the breakfast table, dressed in my usual jeans and sweater. My long straight hair was in braids. I had barely sat down when my mother repeated the oft-thought phrase from my shower musings to me *verbatim*. And that was when I knew the jig was up. That was when I realized my mother truly spoke with dead people.

It wasn't that I had ever doubted this fact. It was no secret. This knowledge floated like mist in the background of my upbringing, constantly shape-shifting into focus and then receding back into the shadows. It was more the case that I hadn't consciously considered whether my mother's experiences with those on the other side of the veil had anything to do with me. Indeed, it had never occurred to me that she could know precisely what I was thinking, word for word. Did she have some innate ability to know this information, or had some spirit told her? I had no idea. All I knew was this: That moment was the dividing line between the before and the after. It marked the change from life as it had been and life as it was going to be. It was the moment I started to re-examine all of the previous whisperings, one-line comments, and mysterious goings-on of my past. It was the moment my perception changed so that I moved from thinking that these things were just things that my family did to wondering what exactly it was that my family could do.

There have been so many instances of psychic phenomena in my life that it is hard to remember them all. These experiences were so pervasive in my life growing up that I never questioned if they were common to others. It never occurred to me that other families did not have similar life-after-death beliefs. I never wondered if the adults in other families could have a cup of tea without searching for meanings in the leaves left in the cup. It wasn't until my father sat down with a deck of playing cards and proceeded to foretell the future for a girlfriend and me that I got an inkling that perhaps, just perhaps, these sorts of occurrences did not happen in my friends' houses.

In short, my parents were Spiritualists. In its most basic form, Spiritualism is a religious philosophy and movement. A core belief is that the souls of the dead exist, can communicate with the living, and continue to evolve on the other side. It is also a religion when Spiritualists band together for spiritual practice. The religion has only seven principles—a belief in a higher power (Spirit, or God, if you prefer) and few tenets beyond the brotherhood of man and personal responsibility. Their belief in the continued existence of the human soul dramatically separates a Spiritualist service from any other religious service. For, at a certain point in a Spiritualist service, a medium gives evidence of life after death from a soul in the spirit ("spirit" with a small "s") world to people in attendance and relays healing messages to them. The messages come from the spirits of loved ones who have passed on. This process is known as mediumship. Both my mother and her sister, Maidi, could do it. To my knowledge, neither of them did it for anyone outside the family. At least one of my father's sisters could do it too. It was decades before I realized I could do it too.

My mother was a young woman in Glasgow during World War II. She was proud of herself for getting excused from assignment to a munitions factory to work in a fish shop instead. That job gave her access to food, not only to add to the meager rations granted to the family but also to use as a form of currency on the black market. She never forgot her tears as she once watched her one rationed poached egg slip off a spoon and slide down the drain. She told of grabbing her gas mask and running for the shelters when the bombers came up the River Clyde to destroy the shipyards. She described the fear of it such that it was palpable in the room all those years later. And she looked back in wonderment at the night she slept through such an air raid in her bed when the sheer exhaustion of surviving took its toll on her. She never forgot the tears, desperation, and brave face she had to put on when the last vestiges of her family were torn apart as her younger brothers were evacuated to the Scottish Highlands for safety. She had hated waiting for letters full of blacked-out content from her young husband, sent from who knew where and mailed who knew when. She had dreaded waiting for news for years after her older brother went missing in North Africa. Always waiting . . . always dreading.

She was, understandably, a no-nonsense realist who got on with the task at hand, whatever it was. And she shared her litany of life lessons to ensure we, too, took a realistic view of the world with us as we went forward in life. I can still hear her thick Scottish brogue as she declared:

"If you think things are tough for you, take a look around, and it willnae be long before you see someone much worse off than yourself."

Or, "If you need a hand, look at the bottom of yer ain sleeve first."

In other words, pity parties were not indulged, and learning self-reliance was mandatory. I cannot thank her enough for instilling these attributes into my persona. Embracing these mantras, and similar others, enabled me to survive much of what life has dealt me.

As for my father, he was a British Royal Navy man for twelve years. He spoke of the years before the war and the countries he had seen as if he had been on some grand touring adventure. But his memories of the war years were his and his alone. A few slipped through, but not many. Only once did he mention the time his ship was torpedoed and sunk in the Mediterranean. He described swimming for twenty-four hours while attempting to dodge the machine-gun fire cutting through the water, water that was on fire. He had believed he was going to die. He remembered all of that very clearly, and yet, he had no memory of being rescued by an allied naval vessel before waking up in a straitjacket in a hospital in Egypt.

Oddly, my father was the softer of my parents. I don't recall him ever raising his voice to me. He would chat lovingly to his hunting dog while adding a raw egg to its dinner because he maintained it was good for the dog's coat. A staunch provider, he was a man who would pour his hot tea onto a saucer to cool it so he could drink it faster so as not to be late for work on a construction site. He would say with all seriousness that "Canada has two seasons, July and winter." And then he would laugh.

Neither of my parents had an easy life. My mother was a city girl, and my father was a country boy, but they were raised through similar hard-scrabble times where luxuries were very few and far between. They were both affected to their cores by the events of the war. My father was discharged from the Navy several years after the war ended. My parents immigrated to Canada with several of my mother's siblings. They came full of hope for a fresh start and the promise of a better life. They also came laden with grief. My mother's youngest brother had died in an accident; a child run over in the street by a truck. Her mother had survived the war only to have her broken heart give out after it ended. My aunt Maidi had buried her baby girl, a toddler dead from meningitis. My father carried his own losses. Both his father and a younger sister had been taken too soon. But still, they all came in search of better times ahead. It was not to be.

Within months of my mother eagerly stepping off an ocean liner in Montreal with her two kilt-clad boys in tow, there was a car accident. My aunt Maidi's husband died at the scene. My mother's two brothers and father (my grandfather) were injured. My aunt spent the next six months in a hospital recovering. My three-year-old cousin came to live with us, clutching a blood-drenched teddy bear in his tiny hand. But those that remained banded even more tightly together, if that was possible.

My aunt eventually came out of the hospital. Her brothers and father closed ranks around her and my cousin. My parents moved to the United States. But they were barely there a year when my eldest brother Ian was diagnosed with a brain tumor. It was two years of chaos and anticipatory grief before he died. My other brother and I were sent to live with my aunt. My father worked any and all overtime to pay for around-the-clock nurses and medical care. My mother chased new treatments from Ontario to Texas and back again, often with her brothers along for the ride. It was all to no avail. My parents lost their house in foreclosure, and on the day Ian died, my parents had less than six dollars between them. A local service club took up a collection and gave them $187. It was yet another new start.

The original new start on this side of the ocean had seen them all arrive with grief inextricably intertwined in their lives. However, they were all still holding onto hope and trying to look forward. But the events of the initial years in this new land changed them all forever. Their hearts were truly and utterly shattered. Grief took up residence in our family. The enormity of it cannot be overstated. It was grief never spoken of, grief never expressed. No answers were ever provided, and we children knew better than to ask. Anything shared, and that was precious little, was just accepted. I am sure they felt that any acknowledgment of their grief would have been like letting the genie out of the bottle. They would never have been able to contain it if it got loose. They would never have been able to go on. So, they did what grievers often do; they compartmentalized the pain and turned in to their family.

"All families are dysfunctional. Some are just more obvious than others," a friend once said. I knew what she meant.

My family looked unremarkable from the outside. Still, a closer inspection revealed the damage within. The truth is that any family living with loss upon loss does not operate smoothly. And the loss of children . . . well, there are no words to describe the destruction that remains after that. I am sure that another loss would have destroyed what was left of my parents' hearts. The adults were trying to keep the ship upright. However, the events of the early years impacted all of us. My brother and cousin received professional help to deal with the sudden onset of stuttering and speech impediments. Seven years behind my remaining brother, I was effectively an only child cloistered in a very quiet home. Sometimes there are no words for the sadness that lives within us, so we give the world silence. We all mastered living silently. It was a silence that screamed. But everyone's silence screamed differently. Together, the silence was deafening. But children can adapt to circumstances, often finding security in the familiar. I was that child. I learned to amuse myself and grew comfortable spending time with myself.

As I looked back and examined my life through a lens clouded by my own grief, it came to me that what I thought was going on in my childhood was not, in fact, accurate. At best, the people around me were good actors, and at worse (and more likely), I was oblivious. Perhaps it was a combination of the two.

To be fair, I was hoodwinked from a very early age, when my views were formed through the eyes of childhood egocentricity. Added to that was a certain measure of memory loss, resulting in a child who grew up believing, for example, that her Christmases were merry for all. And to be clear, I grew up thinking they were. But they couldn't have been merry for anyone in the family who had any memory of the past. Indeed, they were likely not merry for anyone but me after my second birthday.

I was two when my brother was diagnosed with cancer. Two years later, in November, my parents had their final family Christmas with him. (It was spectacular by all accounts.) As expected, he died before the calendar turned to December. I remember none of this. I do not remember him. I do not remember anything of my childhood before the age of seven when my grandfather died. I suspect this is likely because my grandfather was my haven throughout the illness and the aftermath of the death of my brother.

"Trauma upon trauma," a psychiatrist once told me.

And yet, I still remember the Christmases (the ones I do remember) as being joyous. But really, they could not have been. I recall my teetotaling mother having her annual glass of sherry (rarely two), and now I wonder if she needed it to steel herself for the day. Knowing what I know now about grief, I wonder how she did it. I wonder if that is why my father always did all the cooking on Christmas.

Is that how he got through it, by keeping busy? I am sure it is why my mother capitulated all responsibility for shopping and wrapping when I enthusiastically took it on as a teenager.

And every year, my mother's widowed sister Maidi would arrive on December 24 (her own birthday) and present my mother with a bouquet of giant white chrysanthemums. When she came, my aunt had already been to the cemetery to lay flowers on my brother's and grandfather's graves, as my mother never went. It was beyond routine; it was a ritual. But it was the only mention of what must have been an impossible-to-miss elephant in the room. As such, it was brief. It is far too late now, but I am sorry I was unaware of what might have been happening and what people may have felt. I regret that we never talked about it, that I did not ask the right questions.

It seems incredible to me now that people with such an ingrained belief in life after death did so little to acknowledge those who had passed before us at what can be such a magical and painful time of year. It was not as if my brother and others were not mentioned at other times of the year. However, while most remembrances of lost family members were often recalled with various emotions, including laughter, the memories of my brother were more regularly tinged with sorrow. I often sat in the kitchen sharing a quiet cup of tea with my mother, and she would start to reminisce about my brother. In no time, she would be crying. Because I did not remember him, I had nothing to add to the conversation. I would only listen, merely "holding space" in grief parlance, decades before I knew what that term meant. My first memories of this are as a teenager, meaning she was at least a decade out from his death. But there we were, her crying for the loss of her son; me crying in sympathy for her sorrow. I know now how much she would have needed those moments, how important they would have been to her. It warms my heart to know I was able to have been of service to her in this manner. Unbeknownst to me then, this was good training for me for later in life when I would be presented with opportunities to help many people in similar ways.

As I moved through my teenage years, the counterculture moved through society. The late sixties were a fascinating time to come of age. Rules were broken, information on other lifestyles, cultures, and religions flooded forth, and anything seemed possible. It was a time of personal exploration in a million directions while wearing ribbons in my hair. It was also a time of going to coffee houses and becoming immersed in music, often through the haze of marijuana smoke. I was so busy trying to soak it all in that I paid little attention to the superstitious goings-on in my home. When my father spilled salt (seen as bad luck) and immediately threw some over his left shoulder (for good luck), it was such a common occurrence that it barely registered with me. When I returned from shopping downtown on a Saturday afternoon with a new pair of shoes, I knew better than to place them on the table. All my other purchases could be spread out on the table but not new shoes. New shoes on a table were seen to be a harbinger of death. Absolutely nothing could make my mother yell faster than that action.

The other-worldly experiences in our home were harder to ignore. More than once, I came home to be met with a run-down of where I had been, not as questions but as statements. Bear in mind this was the late sixties, the days of party lines and few-and-far-between buses. There were no cellphones or social media sites to troll for information. And my parents certainly could not afford a private investigator to follow me about to see what I was up to. No, there was no money for that. Nor did they need to do that. Somehow, my mother could "see" exactly where I had been and what I had done. I sometimes wonder if she felt she needed to keep an eye on me in any way she could to ensure they did not lose another child.

The first time it happened, she described a restaurant I had been to. She nailed the location. She told me about the restaurant's interior, from the decor to the design of the coffee cups. I am confident it was not an establishment she would have gone into had she even noticed it. There would have been far too many long-haired boys wearing tie-dyed t-shirts in there for her liking. But there she was, giving me a detailed description of the interior dining space as if she had been sitting across from me on the other side of the booth. Another time, she described the footpaths I had walked on the night before on my way to a particular house. As it happened, those paths were entirely surrounded by buildings, and one would never have known they were there from the streets. Indeed, I had become increasingly familiar with the entire downtown core over several years, and I hadn't known they were there until the night I walked on them.

At the time, I had no idea how she knew these things. Now, however, with the benefit of my experiences with my own spiritual work under my belt, I think she may have been doing a psychic technique known as remote viewing. (Remote viewing is where someone with psychic abilities mentally gets impressions of a distant object.) Suffice to say, we had moved into spookier territory as far as I was concerned. It seemed to me that the more my behavior deviated from the straight and narrow, the more spiritual happenings at home ramped up in tandem. When I met David and finally settled down, so did the spirits. But not completely.

Say a door blew open in another house. It might have resulted in a parent asking, "Who didn't shut the door?" or saying, "Someone shut the door!" However, the same occurrence in our house saw my mother simply go to the door, hold it open for a minute, and quietly say, "Come in." Then she closed the door. And she was serious. She was not fooling around. She held the door open and genuinely welcomed a spirit into the house. So, I just accepted that spirits were living in our house, spirits of dead people. Although, I could not have told anyone precisely whose spirits were there. I suspected one was my grandmother (my mother's mother) from passing comments made by my mother, but beyond that, I was guessing.

Further, in my limited life experience to that point, I had no fundamental understanding of what death entailed. I had never seen a dead body. So it was hard for me to formulate what came after death with any certainty. After all, I did not remember my brother or my grandfather, so their deaths were a blank to me. When my father's mother died, she did so in Scotland. My experience of her death consisted of watching my father answer a late-night phone call, during which he spoke softly until he returned the receiver to its cradle. Then, he sat with his shoulders hunched over like he was turning into himself and wept. The fact was, in my sheltered upbringing, I had never even seen a dead animal. Even my father's hunting spoils appeared in the house already prepped for the roasting pan. But that all changed when I was seventeen.

Craig was a beautiful boy with a late-sixties style of long blond hair resting on the shoulders of the fringed jacket he wore with his jeans. He was the type of boy who turned girls' heads when he passed. He was so lovely and had no idea of his effect on others. He was a gentle soul on the cusp of life. And then he died, playing Russian roulette, an almost impossible feat in Canada, where virtually no one was allowed to own a handgun. He was only seventeen years old, his mother's beloved son.

A friend and I went to the funeral home for the visitation. It was the first time I saw a dead person in a casket. But the boy, as I knew him, was gone. His long hair had been shorn into a brush cut, perhaps because his family had never identified with his hippie lifestyle. More probably, it had been the only way to put some semblance of order to whatever shape his hair had been in when the doctors had finished trying to save him. He was wearing a suit. But, of course, that was how it was done at the time. A lot of makeup had been applied in an ineffective attempt to cover the entry wound on his temple. The grief filling the room was oppressive, softened only by the shock that follows the trauma of loss. It was hard to breathe; it was impossible to speak. The entirety of the situation was beyond dreadful on so many levels. But his family was there, amidst the stench of the flowers, bearing witness to it all because he was their cherished child.

In truth, this boy has haunted my life. I have thought of him often throughout the years, and I always remember him fondly. But in the end, I have never been able to fully come to terms with his death. Despite experiencing many deaths in my own family over my life, I never walked up to another open casket again. Such was the profound impact of this experience upon me.

It was not until nearly fifty years later that I viewed a dead body again. I was terrified, but I willed myself to do it because David was my beloved husband. He lay swaddled in an exquisite quilt. His long white hair curled around his shoulders, and his white beard and mustache were pristine. He looked like Santa Claus taking a nap. It was a fitting display for the love of my life. But I knew he wasn't there. By that point in my life, I had learned enough about Spiritualism from my family and on my own to understand he wasn't on that table. His soul was beside me, holding me up as I looked down at him through my tears.

My husband's death taught me how debilitating a loss could be. It gave me a glimpse into how excruciatingly painful life must be for parents who have lost a child. I don't know how they do it, particularly when they have other children for whom they must present a brave face. I don't know how my parents did it. It's like being dead but also being alive simultaneously, traversing the pathways of life like a ghost. Living in a house of grief was like living in a house made of glass. Despite the fragility of the glass, it was the ultimate transparent barrier. From the outside, it looked like the occupants were living in this world. But in reality, they existed in a parallel world known only to grievers.

Given their gifts, it was not a stretch for my family to reach toward the more familiar souls in the spirit world instead of remaining firmly planted only on this side of the veil. With so many dead, perhaps their only way to survive was an immersion in beliefs and activities that kept the tenuously connected threads to the dead intact. I suspect their faith, practice of Spiritualism, and the use of their psychic and mediumship abilities helped to sustain my parents in their loss.

I am my parents' child. So, it did not surprise me when I searched for comfort in the same place my family had found it. As time passed, it became increasingly clear to me that my own beliefs and capabilities were what would support me in my loss. I realized I needed to embrace my spiritual roots to heal myself.

2. WHAT IS IT, EXACTLY?

Sometimes I just know things.

On the third anniversary of David's death, I looked back at our lives together. There were days when it felt like no time had passed at all and other days when I felt as if I had lived an entire lifetime without him. Most days, I just tried to figure out how to conceptualize all of it.

We had had other three-year periods in our life. But they were more concrete in my mind, and I had known where I was in them because he was with me. The external frameworks of those times were easier to identify and move within compared to this internal framework that I could not quite grasp. The days when I felt so lost outnumbered the ones when I thought I might be gaining the upper hand.

I remembered the first three-year segment of our life as we fell in love. With both of us with nondescript starter jobs and no plans, we'd had youth and vitality and nothing but fun on the horizon. Another three-year span saw us all alone in Vancouver, leaning only on one another and starting to soar. Then came my three years at law school with a toddler. And in the end, my law degree was a genuine team effort as he did more parenting than I did, so I could study. Then there were the three years he raced cars, and I saw more garages and racetracks than I ever knew existed. We each got our turn to pursue our dreams, no questions asked.

And then there was our final three-year segment when we had tired of minding the accumulation of our life together and stored some stuff, sold the house, and went traveling. And it was the best time of all. We lived in a trailer, and he drove 50,000 miles all over North America. I remember explicitly thanking him several times. But I know he had wanted to do it for himself too. He had been in his element! And I knew as we did it that we would never do it again. It just had the feeling of it being a one-chance trip. Somehow, I knew in my soul that we would do it and then it would be over. But I could never put my finger on precisely what would be over. I think my heart knew, but my head did not want to believe it.

Sometimes I think we should never have bought that last house. The one he declared "felt like home" the first time we entered it. The one he enjoyed for a single summer. The one I could never get comfortable in. Perhaps the last three years would have been different if we had just kept moving. Perhaps if we had kept moving, death would never have had the chance to catch him.

Sometimes I get a feeling. We all do. It is called intuition. Intuition means into you. It's our connection to our own soul. It's the language of the soul, our inner voice. It is how our soul tries to tell us when something is good or bad. In essence, it is inner sensing. It is knowing something even though we do not know why we know it. Although we all possess this ability, many do not recognize it when it happens. For others, we realize that we "have a feeling." Still, we race to apply logic and conscious reasoning to it and talk ourselves out of hearing what it is trying to tell us. Most of us have had an experience where we got a sense of dread before it happened, a feeling we ignored, dismissed, or applied our thought processes over top of it to minimize the threat. And then, after all was said and done, we said something along the lines of "I should have listened to my gut."

People are born knowing. Some of us have a keener sense of it, and others have a lower one. Of course, these categories are irrelevant if we do not acknowledge, even to ourselves, that we heard something. All of us must work at it to varying degrees to recognize what our soul is trying to tell us. We must actively listen to and heed the message if we are to benefit from the warning.

Sometimes, as in the case above, it isn't clear what the warning is all about. I could never quite put my finger on what would end or how. Was it the traveling, our life together, our lives period? I just could not get a handle on it. And because I could not determine the issue, I could not formulate a response. I would just get the occasional flash of insight that when we stopped moving, something else would stop too.

There are several other ways to experience intuition besides a flash of insight. It can present as an emotional feeling, such as a sense of dread. Or we can get a physical sensation in the pit of our stomach as if we are going to be sick. One of the most common methods is the occurrence of synchronistic events. These are the moments of inexplicable coincidences; for example, when we think of reaching out to someone, only to have them call us at that exact moment.

Finally, dreams can also be a way to experience intuition. Several months before David died (suddenly and unexpectedly), I had an ominous dream. I stood on a low-lying sandy outcropping on the ocean shore under a steel grey sky full of storm clouds. The sea was murky and churning. Even though I knew it was daytime, everything kept getting darker and darker. The water kept swirling and rising, eventually covering the only road and leaving me stranded on an island of sand, surrounded by water. I woke up with the clear realization that something terrible was going to happen. I just did not know what. My soul was talking to me and telling me I would be alone in a dark period of my life, but I wasn't getting the complete message.

Different methods of neurological classification can yield twenty-one or more senses. But the five senses of hearing, sight, smell, taste, and touch are the most commonly known. These are the body's senses that are attuned to the physical world. However, the sixth sense, or psychic abilities as it is more commonly called, is a power of perception beyond the five physical senses, a sense that attunes to energy. When a person with psychic abilities connects to another person, it is a connection from their soul to the other person's soul. The person with psychic abilities perceives and understands the other's energy by reading their aura (the energy field around the body). This gives them glimpses into that person's past, present, and future.

When David and I moved to Vancouver in the early eighties, we knew virtually no one in the city. Further, it seemed as if everyone we met had also been transplanted into Vancouver from other places. However, a gal I worked with befriended me. She was one of those rare people who was actually born and raised in Vancouver. She still socialized with her childhood friends. I was honored when she asked me to join their monthly card nights. They were fun-filled evenings of eating, drinking, and playing cards. The chatter was free-flowing, and I was fascinated by their lives in their European immigrant enclave. They were also like-minded about spiritual matters, and several of them had been to mediums in the past. We didn't play cards at the final gathering before I moved back east. Instead, one girl had arranged for a woman who read tarot cards to come and give each of us a reading.

I must admit, as I pushed open the heavy glass door to the 1940s-style apartment building where she lived, the intrigue was almost as heavy as the door. By the time I reached the marble foyer, I was also excited. I gripped the carved wooden banister for support as I ran up the steps to her apartment. Her home was cozy, made more so when we all squished into the candle-lit living room. The air seemed to be crackling with all the nervous energy charging about. At precisely seven o'clock, there was a knock on the door. Cassandra, the tarot card reader, had arrived.

In no particular order, we each excused ourselves to the bedroom for our one-on-one readings in private. When it was my turn, I noticed a couple of chairs had been set up with a little table beside the bed. The table was covered with a paisley silk scarf. On top of the scarf lay some paper, a pen, a tape recorder, and a deck of tarot cards. She motioned for me to sit down and asked me to shuffle the cards, and as I did so, she introduced herself. Then she took the freshly shuffled cards from me, pushed the "record" button on the recorder, and began. Cassandra selected card after card and placed them face up on the scarf, and as she did so, she talked of many things.

"You are going to move quite far away, back east, I would say. And you are doing this soon, in the next few months," she said. "Actually, you need to be there at a certain time as you are going back to school." This was true; my first year of classes commenced in Toronto in three months.

"You will never be wealthy, but nor will you be poor. You will always have enough money for your needs and a little bit more," she said. So far, this has been the story of my life financially speaking. I do not expect it to change.

What she said next took my breath away, for she put words to a feeling I have had my entire life.

"You are not comfortable on this earth plane," she said. "You sit back and observe. It's like when you go into a movie theatre and sit in the back row, in the aisle seat, so you can see the whole theatre before you." As she spoke, I saw David and me on all those date nights at the movies. We would purposefully go at times when we knew the theatre would be relatively empty. We would enter the

19

theatre and choose the aisle seats on one side of the theatre or the other. And it was always in the very back row. Her description of my actual behavior was striking. I have always felt more like an observer than a participant in life on this earth.

Most of what she said that night was true or came to be confirmed as time passed. Her accuracy was quite remarkable. This was a typical psychic reading. Cassandra perceived information from my energy, using her psychic abilities to tell me what she saw. The fact that she was using a tool that tells a story, such as tarot cards, was simply her working method. She interpreted the tarot cards with the information she was psychically picking up from me. There are many ways to use various tools with psychic abilities. For example, palmistry, which can be found in many cultures worldwide, involves studying the palm of a hand to tell someone's future. Similarly, tea leaf reading consists of interpreting the symbology of the shapes seen and their placement in the teacup to foretell events.

One tool a person can use to tap into their own energy and abilities, to discover something about themselves, is a pendulum. A pendulum is a weighted object suspended on a cord or chain. It is a divination tool in that the pendulum acts as a receiver and transmitter as it taps into the person's intuition and sixth sense. It is used to gain insight into future events. I did this when I was pregnant with my son in the days before the ultrasound was adopted as the way to determine the gender of babies. I suspended a needle on thread above my baby bump, asked the question, and watched to see if the needle swung in circles (for a girl) or back and forth (for a boy). It swung back and forth. And as I did this, I got a quick flash of seeing my father throw salt over his shoulder. Superstitions and old wives' tales, I thought, but were they? Some yes, perhaps, and some no. In any event, it seemed the apple did not fall far from the tree. I was my father's daughter, tuning into my intuitive and psychic energy to determine whether I should buy blue or pink baby pajamas.

So, to be clear, intuition is where our soul talks to us. Psychic ability is where our energy connects to another person's energy, and we perceive information about them. Lastly, mediumship is where our energy connects to the energetic frequencies that are a soul's essence of someone in the spirit world, and we receive information from them. Hence, the word medium; a medium is the means through which a spirit in the spirit world can communicate with a person here on earth.

In essence, the medium receives information from a spirit they have connected with on the other side of the veil. The medium then communicates that to someone here on the earth plane (a "reading"). The medium brings through evidence of the spirit, as that spirit presented when they were on earth. This allows the person receiving the reading (the "sitter") to recognize the identity of the spirit coming through. The medium proves they have contact with whoever they are saying they have contact with by providing the information. Often, a piece of the evidence supplied will be something no one else knows. Sometimes, specific information shows the spirit is aware of an upcoming family celebration and says they will be there. Taken as a whole, it is evidence that indicates that life continues after death.

The second part of the reading is where the medium conveys the message from the spirit. The message is the point of the reading. It is why the spirit came. Spirits do not come because we want them to or to entertain us. They come to tell us something they feel we need to hear. Occasionally, they may tell us that the long-lost key to the safety deposit box is in the top drawer of the old desk in the attic. But more commonly, they come to assure us they transitioned to the spirit world fine and are with other family members who have passed over.

Additionally, they may provide a message of support, give us encouragement, or express their continuing love for us. This is the part of a reading that people find most healing. This is why most grievers who receive readings from a medium report that it comforted them. This is their confirmation that not only does life continue after death, but also that the spirit can communicate with us after the death of the physical body.

In addition to my mother, my aunt was a medium, too. And, through her, the spirits on the other side would talk to my mother. Then my mother would come home and discuss it with my father. Growing up, I overheard many hushed conversations between my mother and father. She never told me what was said, except once. And it was only because I accidentally walked in on the conversation that she told me at all. She said the spirits came "to calm her down and take away her anger." This was completely believable. My mother, a fiery redhead at all times, was at that point in her life no doubt operating on her last nerve. There had been too many deaths, family crises, and money concerns. And, of course, there was always the constant ache in her heart for her boy. In addition, she was enduring her brother's pending death, which was an agonizing replay of her son's passing. She needed these spiritual connections to keep going to get out of bed and put one foot in front of the other. However, it seemed that those on the other side of the veil were monitoring her closely too. She was calmer for quite a while after that night. Whether she was calmer because some healing was done to calm her down or whether it was the result of simply connecting with her loved ones in this manner, I don't know. I just know whatever it was, it worked.

Many years later, I was at a mediumship demonstration in a hotel. There were about eighty people at it. The medium suddenly started to talk.

"I have a mother coming through," she said. "She is looking to connect with her daughter. This daughter lived with her as an adult. The daughter had control over her estate. Everything was to be divided evenly between the daughter and the son, and the daughter did that to the penny. She was pleased by that."

It was my mother. I knew it as soon as the medium mentioned the daughter living with the mother as an adult, for when David and I had returned from Vancouver to Toronto, we had moved in with my mother for several years. This type of very specific evidence makes everyone else in the room know this spirit has not come to communicate with them. The fact that the remainder of the evidence was true confirmed that the medium definitely had connected with my mother. But then came the message.

"She says she was pleased it gave you a leg up in life," the medium said.

My parents never had much, but they worked hard and made the most of what they had. My mother had left my brother and me a modest inheritance each. I was the executor of her estate, and I had made sure it was divided right down the middle. And yes, the money helped me. But hearing her say she was pleased helped me more. It was unbelievably comforting to know that she had seen that I had followed her wishes and that she was happy about that. I came out of the demonstration feeling quite comforted.

Two more ways spirits can communicate with us aside from through a medium are in our dreams and by showing us signs. Two weeks after David died, I went to a small beach town. After lunch, a friend and I toured the town and ended up at the marina. I drank in the sunshine, blue skies, and the sight of boats bobbing gently on the water. It had been the highlight of my post-loss life. And that night, David came to me in a dream for the first time. I dreamt we were sitting in his truck at a marina. We were sitting as we always did, him in the driver's seat and me in the passenger seat. I knew how much he loved his truck, and we had lived in it for the prior three years while traveling. But I had been contemplating selling his truck. To say I was conflicted over this decision might have been the understatement of the century. So, in essence, to this point, the dream made sense to me.

But then he turned, looked at me, opened the door, and got out. I did the same. It was just as we had done thousands of times before. Except this time, I knew he was walking away from his truck. And he was doing it easily, without a second thought. I knew somehow that this was a message for me—that I, too, should let it go.

He never spoke to me or touched me. I am not even sure if he smiled. He just stood and looked at me over the truck's box—and *I have never felt so loved*. I felt the immense heat of it coming from him, the gentleness and peacefulness of it, and the all-encompassing pervasiveness of it, whatever *it* was. *It* felt so wonderful, unlike any sensation I had ever felt in my entire life. *It* was, in a word, "otherworldly."

Just go with *it*, go with him, I thought. And I immediately understood why people are drawn to and go to the light.

This dream was definitely a communication from David wherever he was on the other side. It had a three-fold message. The first was that he knew what I was up to. Placing us at the marina was enough to tell me that. Secondly, he let me know it was okay for me to sell his truck. That message was a huge comfort to me. David had been a car guy all his life, and his vehicles had been his pride and joy. But when I watched him just walk away from it in the dream, all of the conflicts about that decision left my being. The third part was his message to me that he still loved me. He confirmed that the heart may stop beating, but it does not stop loving. Many times in my grief journey, I have clung to this.

Spirits also communicate with us by sending us signs. If we are aware and paying attention, these events can lead to wake-up calls, messages received, or simply the feeling that we are not alone. I always take notice of the dimes I find in unusual places. I read their dates to see if that year was special to me for any reason. When I find a feather in a place where no feather should be, I think of my loved ones. When the scent of my mother's perfume comes at me from out of nowhere, I acknowledge her presence. For they are telling me that they are thinking of me. They are letting me know they are watching me. I take comfort in the knowledge that they are with me.

One day last winter, I contemplated taking flowers to the cemetery for my mum and David's mum. But there was a fine layer of ice and snow on the ground, and it was hard to find their plots on a sunny summer day. There are no headstones. Only plaques flush with the ground are allowed. So, instead, I ordered a floral arrangement for my house. It was easy enough to do with online shopping and all, until I could not click past the section asking what message I wanted to be written on the accompanying card. I could hardly address a card to me, and I live alone. So I typed in *Merry Christmas, sweetie xo*. It seemed appropriate. After all, he rarely called me anything else. And it got me past that section to complete the order.

When I unwrapped the flowers, I immediately discarded the card into my recycle box. I didn't need a card from me to me, I thought. The next day was garbage pick-up day, and something caught my eye as I retrieved the emptied bins from the lawn. It was the card. The card was lying alone in the grass. I could have assumed it had just fallen out during the emptying process. But how it managed to be the only item left behind from the midst of all the paper in that box stymied me. So, I chose to believe David made sure it was left there for me to retrieve. I put it back in the flower arrangement to imagine him saying, "Merry Christmas, sweetie xo," to me throughout the holidays. It felt like the right thing to do, uplifting my spirits every time I looked at it. It reinforced my belief in the afterlife whenever my eyes landed on it.

People who have lost a loved one are vulnerable. Quite simply, we are hurting. After David died, my soul knew something was wrong, and I searched for comfort and respite. I needed to feel held. There was no one better to provide the love I needed than my loved one who had passed. Accepting life after death led me to reconstruct a relationship with David so that I could move forward with a new relationship with him in place. It is not the relationship I preferred. But it was still a relationship. In my view, having a continuing bond with him was preferable to attempting to move on and forget, which I, like most grievers, cannot do. This popular therapeutic approach ("continuing bonds") has been known to positively affect the bereaved.

However, a reading with a medium is also a powerful healing force for easing someone's grief. Spiritualism is all about love, helping people feel better, and healing. The evidence that life continues after death is simply the means to help us understand that our loved ones are still with us, involved in our lives, and sending love and support from the other side. This is why, after David died, I began attending a Spiritualist church regularly and visited the odd medium for a reading. Together, these therapeutic and spiritual approaches complemented one another in a way that facilitated my healing. In other words, combining these methods worked best for me.

3. SAY WHAT?

Sometimes in our lives, we make big decisions and embark on a new journey to make our plans come to fruition. The summer of 1978 was such a time for me. After taking a few years off from college, I enrolled to attend a university in the fall to get a B.A. At the same time, David moved a hundred miles away to finish his apprenticeship. We had plans. In two years, we would be done and on our way.

In numerology, my Life Path number is seven. We sevens are information seekers. We cannot get enough information about anything and everything. So, when my mother casually asked me to accompany her to a psychic fair, I did not have to be asked twice. It was a warm summer night, and I had nothing else on my social calendar. I had no idea what to expect about this outing, but I was curious to see what it was all about. I thought it would be a pleasant way to pass the evening. I was wrong.

As soon as we entered the building on the fairgrounds, I noticed the air was electric. The energy was mounting. Vendors of all manner of psychic and energy paraphernalia like tarot cards, crystals, and jewelry, in addition to those offering healing services like reiki, were ready to work. The clientele was bustling about with expectant anticipation. My mother walked around and perused the offerings to see what spoke to her. This is how it is done. Services or products at these events are selected by what calls to us, not who is closest to the entrance or has the longest line-up. My mother suggested we go into a large room and watch the next scheduled speaker do a psychic demonstration. That seemed like a harmless enough endeavor to me. In my naivete, it never occurred to me that I could get chosen for a reading in this public forum. If it had, I might have begged off as we sevens also have an aversion to the spotlight. I thought since I did not want a reading, I was safe. I was wrong, again.

So there we were, sitting among a hundred or so others, most of whom were anxious to receive a message. On the stage, Simon, from England, started his opening patter, indicating he was a bit of a showman. "Entertaining" was the word that came to my mind. He walked about the stage and then turned and looked at me.

"You are going back to school," he said.

That was true, but I did not even get a chance to answer him before he started talking to another girl sitting four rows in front of me about something in her life.

Whew! I thought. I felt relieved. But it was not to be.

I heard him say to the other girl, "I'm sorry, dear. I will return to you in a minute, but first, we have to get to the scandal!" And he turned back to me. The audience broke out laughing. I did not.

"So you are going back to school," he started again. "You have been away from it for a while. And when you go, you will enter a classroom and sit down. And a man will come in and sit three seats to your left. And you are going to become very close to him."

I was transfixed as I nervously twirled my engagement ring around on my finger.

"You are going to marry a man whose Christian name starts with D," he said, lowering his voice, "but he will not be the same man you are with today."

Fear gripped my heart.

I honestly don't recall what he said after that. I believe he went back to the other girl. I am not really sure. I was too shocked. This man had been right enough about the school information to make me believe he might just be right about the rest of it. And since I had been madly in love with David for the last six years, I was not about to let Simon be right.

I decided that I would change the future as he had foretold it. And so it began. A game of musical chairs was afoot in every classroom I entered. I made it my mission to sit in the last chairs at the end of rows so no one could sit to my left. Not three, two, or even one seat was ever to my left. And for a couple of weeks, I was pretty effective in controlling my environment. Then came the day I went into a laboratory for my geology class. Again, I sat on the last stool of the row of stools. There were no stools to my left. I was pretty pleased with how this was going until a guy walked in and sat down *across* the lab table from me—three seats to my left. It never occurred to me that more stools were on his side of the table than mine.

As it happened, that fellow and I did become close, as close as lab partners can be over a year. But he had a girlfriend, and I had David, so that was all we were. No scandal there. Oh, and the man I married whose name started with D—that was my fiancé, David, but by the time we married seven years later, he was not the same man as he had been on the night Simon talked about him.

"There's many a slip between the cup and the lip," my mother used to say.

She was saying that a lot can happen between our plans and the ultimate result. This is not only true regarding events in life in general, but it is also true for the information being given by a psychic or medium during a reading. That reading taught me that caution should always be the order of the day when listening to what someone tells me in these circumstances.

To begin with, the person doing a reading (the "reader") relays the information as they perceive or receive it. The reader may not understand the information as they get it. Or they may misinterpret it. Or they may, in their attempt to convey the information, characterize it wrong or present it in a not entirely clear manner. Sometimes they can state something inaccurately because whatever they are trying to say is something too far off into the future, so they cannot see it clearly enough. This last one is particularly true if the reading is a psychic reading, like the one from Simon. He got the immediate future events pretty clear. Still, the point about who I would marry was an event seven years into the future. It was obviously less clear to him, leading him to misconstrue the more recent events as having more validity than they merited. He may also have gotten a little carried away by his flair for the dramatic.

In addition, there are many ways to interpret what we hear being said. Sometimes a reader may be saying something entirely accurate, but it isn't what we want to hear. Perhaps we came seeking information about one aspect of our life, and they are talking about another. We may not be listening as attentively as we should be and thus, come away with the wrong impression of what was said. Or the reader may be saying something, again entirely accurate, but we don't want to hear it for one reason or another. So again, we don't fully listen to what they are saying. Readings are populated by people whose emotions are often very close to the surface. Therefore, it is not unusual for the ego to get in the way of what is heard.

Sometimes the information is too vague, leaving us to fill in the blanks, and we can do that incorrectly. Sometimes it is of little consequence; other times, it is not. I recall the tarot card reader in Vancouver telling me I would have a difficult relationship with a female in-law. She hesitated as she said she thought it was my mother-in-law. She clearly wasn't sure. I couldn't understand it as I adored my mother-in-law. I forgot about it. It wasn't until years later, as I reviewed my relationship with my sister-in-law that I realized it had always been her. As if I had needed any more confirmation that I was correct, when that realization hit, I immediately remembered my father's succinct characterization of her from many years prior.

"God Almighty couldn't please that one," he had said. He had been right.

Other times, the information presented can be vague but be presented quite confidently. It may or may not be good news, but in such circumstances, we may rush to make sense of it, often blindly rushing in the wrong direction. For example, my mother went for a psychic reading while my father was working away from home at a nuclear plant, a location he did not like. The psychic said he saw a man being carried out of a plant with cables hanging overhead. My mother came home very upset. She worried every day my father went to work that he would not come home at night. Less than two weeks later, my mother's brother collapsed at work in an automotive plant where he had worked for over twenty years. He had an undiagnosed brain tumor. My mother was totally blindsided. She was so busy looking left that she never saw what was coming from the right. My personal view is that this should not have happened. Partial information like this should never have been provided to my mother since it was more likely to negatively impact her than not.

However, my mother was no stranger to receiving distressing news in readings. I don't know whether she asked for candor or the readers could not control their filters in her presence. Perhaps when one has as many readings as she had in her life, it is simply the odds. They can't all be good, right? Still, I think serious consideration should be given to presentation if bad news is seen. And since no one knows the details of deaths in advance, there should be no disclosures given to anyone in that regard, ever. Consider the following. When my mother gave birth to my eldest brother, she was a serviceman's wife living with her parents in wartime. Several days after the birth, my grandmother's best friend came to see the new baby. As was the custom, she took my brother in her arms and crossed his tiny palms with silver for good luck. She studied him.

"He's a bonny one, Flora, but he's not long for this world," she said.

"Don't say that," my grandmother protested.

But the words were out. My mother stood off to the side as another of her sayings reverberated through her brain. If it's for ye, it'll no go by ye, she thought.

And indeed, this did not pass her by as my brother died before his twelfth birthday.

My parents always stressed that even if there may be a master plan for our lives, we always have free will. It may have been one way of keeping hope for the future instead of resigning themselves to fate. Of course, that was what I tried to do with my musical chairs shenanigans, to no avail. The more powerful lesson for me was that sometimes we can't stop what is coming, no matter how hard we try. But sometimes, knowing what may be coming down the road of life can make a difference. And that was the objective on one otherwise ordinary night in my late teens.

It was an exciting time in that tiny kitchen with its Harvest Gold appliances, linoleum floor, and metal teapot constantly on the lowest setting on the stove. Teenage schoolgirl enthusiasm filled the air. It was the night my father had finally succumbed to weeks of pestering on the part of my bestie Carol and myself. He was going to read our cards. Tell our futures. Hopefully, tell us about romantic interests yet to come. It didn't entirely turn out like that.

Now, my father could read people psychically as they sat at the kitchen table drinking tea. No tarot cards or crystal balls were required. And he never did it for money or entertainment. Instead, he was quiet about his abilities and usually only shared them with my mother. But as we girls had become increasingly aware of his gift, we wanted to see it in action, and truth be told, we had our own agenda.

So we sat down that evening, and he started shuffling a deck of regular playing cards. I know now that he did not need any props at the time. He told us later that as far as he was concerned, those items were purely for our benefit. Certainly, the cards rendered an atmosphere of legitimacy to the entire event. We were riveted to find out what life held for us.

He started with Carol. He turned over a few cards.

"You will end up with a man with dark hair. His Christian name will start with the letter P," he said.

We were confused. We only knew one man in her life that fit that description, and he was a good friend but nothing more. She went on in life to marry a man whose first name did not start with a P. But it was short-lived, and after divorcing him, she met Peter, a dark-haired man with whom she has spent nearly four decades of her life. So, my father's reading was accurate, but it took some years to pass before we could see the truth of what he saw for her.

When it was my turn, he turned over a few more cards.

"You will be a long time leaving home, and when you do, you will move very far away . . . I would not rule out Australia," he said.

As it happened, I did not move out of my parents' house for another decade. When I did, I moved 2600 miles away to Vancouver, British Columbia. Interestingly, despite being very well-traveled, I have never been to Australia. I almost made it once. On our honeymoon, David and I flew out of Vancouver with tickets to Fiji and Australia. But after two weeks of sand, surf, and sun in Fiji, we discovered we did not have the proper visas to be admitted into Australia. Hours later, we caught the jetliner on its way back north, got off the plane in Hawaii, and spent two weeks there instead. So, many years later, I looked at what he had said that night and said to myself, "Long time leaving, *check*. Moving very far away, *check*. Australia, *hmm . . . interesting.*"

Sometimes having a little knowledge can be, as they say, dangerous. And sometimes, we simply don't want to face what the reader may say. The presence of either of these attitudes (or both together) can lead to events unfolding in a less than flattering way. I will never forget my worst reading.

In 2008 I stood in Mallory Square in Key West. It was a spot where every evening, people gathered to watch the sun plummet into the horizon. The Sunset Celebration was a street party. People in t-shirts and sundresses ambled about with drinks in their hands. At the same time, they listened to music, perused vendors' wares, and watched buskers. I saw a man offering tarot card readings. David had gone to buy something, so I thought I had time to get a quick reading while on my own.

I laid down his fee while the man shuffled the cards. Then, he placed six cards down on the table in a pattern. I knew virtually nothing about tarot cards, but a feeling of dread entered my stomach. My intuition was on high alert. David and I had been going through some challenging times, and when I saw these cards splayed out on the table, I knew that those times were what was being shown to me. It took me nary a second to recognize the Four of Cups, the Three of Swords, the Tower, and the Lovers among the cards he had laid down. The Four of Cups, in this context, was contemplation. The Three of Swords was heartbreak or grief. The Tower indicated sudden, unwanted change. And the Lovers identified the people involved. The man started to speak, but I didn't want to hear it. I figured I already had a fair idea of what he would say. I began to walk away quickly as he pleaded with me to stop and listen to him. He was clearly concerned.

"Don't worry about me. I will be fine," I called back to him.

I don't think he believed me. I probably would not have believed me either if I had been him. I can't even say with certainty that I even believed myself. However, this happened because I let my fears consume me. Possibly, he would have told me some good news, but I did not give him a chance to tell me what he saw. Indeed, I did not get the whole message. I fled with my own incomplete view in my head. But there is always a choice in life, and once again, I was going to exercise my free will to change whatever outcome had appeared in those cards.

There are energetic cords to every relationship in life; positive, negative, and neutral. Care must be taken to recognize when cords may become more like a rope and, thus, may need to be dealt with. When cutting negative cords, the point is to cut the cord, send energy back to the other person, and reclaim our energy. This results in reclaiming one's own power. We can cut cords to all sorts of things, such as books not read, a closet not cleaned, or parts of our lives. The intensity of the relationship dictates the cord's intensity. I decided that this was how I would deal with the situation highlighted in the Key West tarot cards.

There are many ways to cut cords, including meditation, resonant sound therapy, or ritual. I remember once that a friend sat in a car in my driveway doing this. Her first love had tracked her down after twenty years and just happened to catch up with her when she was back in the province visiting. He believed a Karmic debt was owed, which he felt needed to be released. He performed a ritual with her that involved a ribbon to tie their hands, a book, and some prearranged words. So, it is possible to do it on one's own, but sometimes, a skilled healer is required to ensure support in the complete severing of the cord and the healing of the wound.

In my case, I sought help. I attended a conference in a convention center full of speakers, vendors, and practitioners of all kinds of spiritual and energy work. However, it wasn't until I read the event brochure that I noticed a woman offered cord-cutting services. Perfect, I thought. I had not gone looking for this particular service, but it was right in front of me. I decided to give it a try. I wanted to eliminate the negative energy emanating from the aforementioned challenging times between David and me. I booked a fifteen-minute appointment for 3:00 p.m. I was there on the dot.

She did it in a hallway with other attendees moving to and fro. She set up two chairs just off to the side of the corridor, out of the flow of the pedestrian traffic. I was captivated by her presence from the moment I sat down. Despite the hustle and bustle, I felt alone with her in a silent bubble. She took my hands and talked me through a meditation that included a visualization of actually cutting the cord that carried the negative energy. By the end of the session, I felt better. Later that evening, I told David about it. But I never mentioned the actual time she did it, as it seemed irrelevant. He set his coffee cup down and just looked at me.

"You did that at ten after three," he said. "I was riding the bike then, and I felt it. I didn't know what it was . . . what was happening. I looked at my watch to note the time. But it was quick, and then it was gone."

"That is exactly right," I said.

I was too stunned to talk about it further. But I thought that was the last time I would ever do something like that without knowing where the other person was and what they were doing. My actions could have caused him to have an accident or worse. The lesson: we must be careful when we undertake energy work involving another person.

There is a medium for every spirit in the spirit world, but not every medium can work with every spirit. It may be that the medium is feeling less than a hundred percent able to work for physical or emotional reasons. Mediums are, after all, people too. Or they may be unable to work with the spirit that comes through. They might not be able to fit with the energy. The fact is the spirits are in control. They determine who needs to come through and why. It is not up to the medium or the client. Similarly, the medium may not be able to work with the client. Clients show up with their own needs, wants, and agendas. They usually know who they want to hear from and may not be happy to hear from someone else. An awkward situation can arise if the spirit trying to come through was someone the client disliked on earth. No matter how distasteful the person may have been when on the earth plane, they only come through on a vibration of love once they have passed over. But that does not mean the client is ready to hear from them.

The inability to complete a session occurred with my mother when I lived in Vancouver. My mother came to visit after my father had passed away the previous year, and she was in the throes of grief. I knew a well-known local medium and thought a session with him might help her. It was one of those rare West Coast days where the sky was blue, and the sun was shining. Tiny whitecaps in the bay reflected the light like prisms. It seemed almost magical. The sight of the North Shore Mountains was breathtaking. And as usual, they made me feel grounded and insignificant in the world. That sort of day always confirmed the belief that something bigger than us was at play, and one just needed to flow with it. I made sure we had lots of time to soak up the journey on the way to his home.

I was excited when I pulled up to the brick ranch-style house on a suburban street. I parked the car, and we carefully navigated the walk across his cobblestone driveway. He was waiting at the open front door and graciously ushered us inside. Classical music softly drifted through the house. Beethoven? I was sure it was Beethoven. He led us to a plush oversized sectional sofa in front of a huge window. It overlooked the bay. A box of tissues sat discreetly on the antique end table, within easy reach. He provided my mother with a cup of tea. When she was comfortably settled to his satisfaction, he led me to his office a few yards away. My session progressed as expected. When we had finished, he provided me with a cup of tea, and I took my mother's place on the sofa. She went with him to his office. They were not gone long. After what seemed to be only a few minutes, the door to the office flew open, and the medium moved swiftly into the hall. He held his head with both hands as he swept past me and down another hallway. Towards a bedroom, maybe?

"Too strong. Too strong," he muttered as he passed.

It was several more minutes before he reappeared. He apologized for being unable to complete my mother's session. She did not seem surprised. My mother took it in her stride as if this had happened to her before. When I asked her about it later, she told me that he had said she "was too strong for him to work with." She may also have been one of those clients with their own agendas, but one with some of her own abilities to back it up, making his work impossible. A third option that came to mind was that perhaps my brother had presented to the medium by revealing the pain in his head as he died. The medium was not a robust fellow, and it may have been too much for him to bear.

So, although it is rare, a medium may be unable to continue with or complete a session for many reasons. However, in any of these circumstances, there is an opportunity for the ethical medium to refund any monies paid. Then, they can either reschedule the appointment or wish the client well on their next attempt with someone else. Of course, the way to lessen the chances of this happening is to choose a very experienced medium. The professional medium has honed their craft and therefore is more likely to have the increased accuracy that comes from experience and the necessary physical stamina to perform the reading.

When it comes to psychics and mediums, and related spiritual beliefs, there are believers, skeptics, non-believers, and people for whom belief in them does not matter one way or the other. For many years, I never knew where David fell on this continuum. We didn't talk about it. I would tell him of the latest occurrence in my life concerning this realm. He would listen, but he never indicated whether he believed as I did or if the fact that I believed was enough for both of us. At best, I felt he was someone for whom it did not matter one way or the other. And then, as the clock approached midnight one Saturday night, he used my own beliefs to comfort me.

My father had been dead almost two years when I gave birth to our son. The process started on a Friday afternoon. I went to a regularly scheduled doctor's appointment. He told me to go home, pack my toothbrush, and check in to the local maternity hospital. The following morning at eight o'clock, I was taken to a dimly lit private birthing room. A nurse gave me a drug to induce delivery. I spent the next twelve hours in the quiet with a midwife and a nurse at my side, willing it to work. Other staff occasionally bustled in and out. Several doctors checked on me. It did not work. In the early evening, the decision was made to perform a Caesarean section. Suddenly, everyone was moving very quickly, and there was noise everywhere. The operating room lights glared harshly. I was freezing. I thought I was shivering. I saw the concern on the midwife's face as she strapped my arms down. She explained to me that I was starting to convulse.

"You'll be fine," she said. Everything went dark.

When I woke up later, I was in another silent dimly lit room. I felt like I was enveloped in a soft cocoon. Everything looked fuzzy around the edges. David was standing, looking down at me. Through my morphine haze, I wasn't sure if he would faint or throw up. But as soon as I focused on him, he seemed to brighten.

"Have you seen him?" he said softly. "He's beautiful. He is wearing a little blue hat."

I couldn't even nod. He chattered on about how amazing it was that I had had our son on the twenty-third day of the month. David, his father, and his brother were all born on the twenty-third of different months. I had trouble staying with him. I kept drifting in and out. It might have been the mention of the family that did it, but I was suddenly overwhelmed with sadness. My lips quivered and tears fell from the corner of my eyes.

"I wish my dad could see him," I said. I said it so quietly that I was not even sure David had heard me.

David wiped the tears from my face as he leaned down to whisper in my ear. He had heard me. And he didn't miss a beat in responding.

"He sees him, sweetie, he sees him," he said.

And from that moment on, I knew David believed in all of it too. He had answered too fast, as if from instinct, seemingly without even considering his response. At the very least, he knew what I believed and needed to hear. He may have chosen to validate my own beliefs to soothe me.

Even though there are times when the spoken word is a source of comfort and healing, there are other times when what is said may be misinterpreted, misconstrued, or inaccurate. We need to know which is which, for blind faith in what is said to us is perilous in any part of our lives. *Caution* should always be the watchword when dealing with information received in readings.

4. HEALING

When David moved to another city to complete his apprenticeship training, it was a two-year commitment to the finish line. Although I had started a three-year degree, I had opted to cram it into the same two years. I went to school fulltime but also took summer school and intercession courses. I even took a second-year course in my first year at the same time I was taking its first-year prerequisite course. By the end of my final year, I was an emotional mess.

David's absence had untethered me. While I was desperate for his phone calls, they were but momentary respites. Weekend visits had morphed from excited reunions to my suffering full-blown anxiety attacks when we met. In addition, my uncle was dying. He had the same glioblastoma that killed my eldest brother as a child. Naturally, my mother and my aunt were reeling. It was as if there was no solid footing anywhere in my life. I was still on the Dean's List, but only because I kept bi-monthly appointments with a psychiatrist and consumed up to eight tranquilizers a day. But I kept moving. It was all I knew to do. For in my house, that was the way it was done. One foot was put in front of the other, no matter what.

One night, near the end of my final course, my mother and I visited my aunt. I thought we went just to check in on her and my uncle and lend some support, the usual reasons one sees relatives when someone is ill. But looking back on the events of that night, that was probably not the purpose of the visit at all. When we arrived, my uncle was sleeping. My mother and aunt went into the living room and closed the door. I sat at the dining room table and took out a textbook and highlighter. I couldn't concentrate. I listened to the soft music emanating from the phonograph in the other room. Were they whispering? Why couldn't I hear their conversation? Neither of them would have been called "soft-spoken" by anyone. In my soul, I knew something was going on in that room, something that had to do with their abilities. But I had no idea what. And I made no effort to find out. Indeed, it seemed as if I could not have moved from my chair if I had wanted to.

I knew my mother could put my aunt into a trance by playing a specific piece of music and doing or saying who knows what. It was one way she communicated with those on the other side of the veil. This process had simply been stated as a fact at some point in my upbringing. But my intuition told me that when that door opened, I was about to get a ring-side seat to the entire performance. Moreover, I feared I would be a significant player in this scene.

Time passed, and mounting fear continued to rivet me to my chair. Then the door opened. My mother and my aunt walked toward me slowly. Something was off. I could feel it. I ran to the kitchen. I should have turned right, I thought. The back door was right there! But in haste and fear, I had backed up against the refrigerator in the corner of her tiny kitchen beside a locked window. I was trapped.

"Your grandfather is here," my mother said.

My aunt started talking. It was her voice, but my grandfather (their father) was the one speaking. He was offering soothing, placating statements to calm me down. I was having none of it.

Finally, my mother interjected again.

"Just let her put her hands on your face," she said. "They just want to take away the pressure." They? Who are they?

My terror was the final straw. It broke me. At that moment, I was no match for any of them individually, and certainly not all of them together. My aunt gently cupped my tear-stained face in her hands. And that is when I felt it. A whoosh of energy moved from the top of my head and drained out of my face through her hands. I felt as if her touch had lifted the weight of the world from my head. Suddenly, there was a fresh emptiness; previously, my brain had felt like it was too full and about to burst. I felt peaceful and calmer, and suddenly there was room in my head to think. The significance of this incident was never lost on me. But it would be several years before I put the name "spiritual healing" to it.

Not surprisingly, when I attended law school a decade later, history repeated itself. By then, I had a toddler underfoot, in addition to a different psychiatrist and more tranquilizers. I held myself together for a long time, but halfway through the second year, I started to fray badly around the edges. When David went away to Chicago on business, I began to crack. My aunt arrived, and as before, I was doing homework. She came in and sat on the bed in my room. She said she had my brother, Ian, with her. I got up and moved to sit on the bed with her. This time I was a willing participant. Indeed, I could hardly wait for her to put her hands on me. This time, my brother came through her to help me. And it worked again, just like the first time.

Now, my healings were hands-on healing experiences. My aunt, in both cases, was the medium, and the spirits worked through her hands on me. This is not a foreign concept to most people. The Bible has numerous examples of Jesus himself doing this. Pentecostals, Baptists, and other Christian faiths utilize the power of healing prayer by laying hands. In a Spiritualist church service, a portion of the service is dedicated to a healing meditation. Those who wish to experience a possible physical transfer of spiritual healing through a medium are invited to sit in a designated church area to receive it.

Intuitive healers work on a similar premise. These are the people in our everyday lives who put their hands on others to comfort, such as a reassuring touch while talking. They may not even be aware they are doing it or why. If asked, they may just say it is a habit. But we all know someone who has offered this sort of healing to us.

Spiritual healers may also use several forms of energy therapies, such as crystal healing, sound therapy, and so on. For example, sound therapy is a form of energy healing that does not require a healer's touch. Sound therapists use sound frequencies to interact with the body's different energy frequencies to balance the body's energy. They do so by using instruments such as tuning forks, chimes, crystal singing bowls, and Tibetan bells, to name a few. This is not music but rather pure sounds. But if one thinks of the uplifting effects of music, it is not hard to imagine the benefits of tinkling bells and singing bowls. The experience can be combined with a meditation that leads the client into a meditative state. My only experience with this sort of session occurred about a year ago when I attended one class purely out of curiosity and interest. It was an online class, and it started with a meditation. Then I heard sounds. The crystal-clear sounds of tinkling bells progressed to more fulsome and deep sounds, eventually reaching a crescendo before easing back to silence. The session lasted seventy-five minutes. I would have sworn it was ten minutes at most. However, without any reservation, I can also say that the experience was one of the top five healing experiences of my life. It was simply incredible.

Reiki is likely the most well-known form of energy healing that may or may not require touch. The healer uses gentle hand move-ments just a few inches above the patient's body in the body's auric field. The intent is to guide healthy energy flow through the body to reduce stress and promote healing. The effects can be emotional, physical, or spiritual. Sometimes, the reiki healer will employ a gentle touch therapy that involves placing their hands on various parts of the patient's body.

In the fall of 2007, I was experiencing some challenges in my personal life. My last surviving brother had died two years prior, and my birth family was gone. David operated his own business and worked overtime at it. I worked long hours as a lawyer for a bank downtown in the city's financial district. The stress was relentless. I noticed tension had settled in my neck and shoulder, on the side where I had suffered a slight whiplash injury a decade before. Stress always seemed to gravitate to this weak spot in my body to cause pain. The pain became excruciating. It also became an everyday occurrence.

A like-minded friend at work suggested I try reiki treatments and gave me the telephone number of a medium she had been to. I called Carolina and set up an appointment. The next day I looked like I was going off to a business meeting in my wool suit and silk blouse. Nothing could have been further from the truth. I was hopeful as I ran down the front steps of the office tower and got in a cab for the quick ride to her downtown office. I entered the small commercial building, and my heels clicked on the linoleum floor as I quickly searched the door numbers. I had no qualms. I believed she could help me. I had had enough mystical experiences in my life to understand that this alternative treatment style might work. Something had to work because self-medicating with painkillers was not an option that would serve me well in the long run.

When I knocked on her door, she opened it, and plumes of smoke emitting from burning sage wafted past me. There was a slight haze in the room. Her tiny office had two comfy wing-back chairs, a massage table, and no end to the sorts of items one would expect to find for sale in a mystical shop. Lotions, oils, crystals, incense, and so on were clearly labeled and neatly arranged on the shelves.

"Come in," she said. "Welcome!" She smiled broadly.

I introduced myself, and after some perfunctory instructions, she immediately set to work preparing the table. I removed my jacket and hung it carefully on the back of her door. She motioned to the table.

"Just lie here," she said.

I did as she directed and lay down on my stomach, with my view consisting only of the threadbare carpet on the floor. Everything was silent. Suddenly, there was a sound. I hadn't been prepared for that. But it was the most precise, purest sound I had ever heard. It spoke to my soul. She had lifted an ornate Tibetan singing bowl, struck it with the padded side of a mallet, and made the bowl sing. Ah . . . what a bonus! She used sound therapy to signal the start of the treatment. A sense of calm overcame me. I was ready to be healed. For thirty minutes, I remained motionless, lying in silence as Carolina's hands moved above various parts of my body. When I eventually got up from the table, the pain in my neck was gone. I was not surprised, and I was grateful.

In my view, mediumship is the ultimate form of non-touch spiritual healing. There are two ways mediumship can be used to heal, which for ease of reference, I will call directly and indirectly. In the direct method, the medium does not give evidence of life after death or a message from a loved one. They do not connect with a loved one at all. Instead, the medium relies on their healing guides to come through them and send healing telepathically to the recipient. It may look like the medium is just sitting still with their eyes closed. But the medium will have entered a meditative state, making it easier for their healing guides to come through. And the healing guides will not only prioritize the part of the body that requires healing but direct the healing to it. And they will also time it for they know how long it is needed. And since no touch is involved, there is no limitation on the distance at which this can be done. Healing energy can be sent from thousands of miles away with the aid of a computer screen, telephone, or nothing at all. Energy follows thought. And the thought of the medium is for the healing guides to send healing. I can personally attest to the fact that this method works.

Last summer, my dog had surgery. I had already been crying for almost two hours by the time I arrived at the animal hospital. For she had been David's dog. To lose her would have crushed me. My brain told me she would be fine, but my heart, well, my heart just couldn't take anymore. It wasn't the surgery that was risky for her but the anesthesia. I had almost lost her the previous year due to her adverse reaction during a minor operation. So the surgeon had arranged for a specialist just for that this time. The internist was so thorough that her email reports made my head spin. And as the veterinary technician went on and on, going through her checklist of things clients must be informed of, I started to tear up again. And then any control I had was gone.

"If it comes to it, do you want us to do CPR on her?" she asked.

I'm sorry . . . what? CPR? And David died all over again in my head. I remembered the reports in my desk detailing how long they gave him CPR. How it didn't work. How it doesn't work anywhere near as well as television would have us believe. How ribs can be broken. How I was afraid to hug him in the funeral home because I was afraid if they had broken his ribs, I would hurt him, even though he was beyond any pain in this world. I was beyond whimpering at this point.

"Are we talking about a DNR for my dog?" I asked.

She confirmed we were. Eventually, I returned to my car and cried until I could pull myself together to drive. It took a long, long time.

I carried the stress of that dog's illness and operation for two months in my lower back. From the first sign of an issue, through diagnostic tests to the scheduling of her surgery, and even after the successful operation, I could barely walk. I pulled myself up the stairs in my house by using the banister while wincing in pain. I consulted my doctor, who advised me that the x-rays of my hips disclosed no issues. I took pain medication. I made sure I had a cane with me for support on my walks with the dog. Although it was summertime, I stood in hot showers and turned on the heated mattress cover before going to bed. I tried everything I could think of. And then I booked an appointment with a medium.

I looked at her on the computer screen. She was on the other side of the Atlantic Ocean. It did not matter. She led me in a meditation, and then we sat in silence. She was just sitting there with her eyes closed. But I knew. Just wait, I thought. And then it started. I felt tingling over my lower back down to the top of my legs. Then I felt the whole area heat up as if someone had put a heating pad on it. I sat there for a long time with my eyes closed, just paying attention to the experience. When she finished, she asked me how it felt. I wasn't sure. I had been so intent on noticing the physical sensations occurring that I hadn't realized what had happened to the pain. Or maybe I did not notice the pain because it was gone! I stood up and walked around the living room, unaided and not feeling searing stabs of pain. I felt so much lighter, almost relaxed. And all the stress and pain in my back were definitely gone. It has never returned.

As effective as direct spiritual healing is, most people will only experience the effects of indirect spiritual healing. Their experience is generally one where they visit a medium for a reading to contact a loved one who has passed. The medium connects with the spirit of their loved one(s) and provides evidence about the spirit communicator so the recipient can determine who is there. Then the medium will give the message from the spirit. This experience can be healing in several ways.

The evidence given by the medium is critical to the success of the session being a healing one. In a successful session, the evidence always shows that the sitter's loved one continues to live on in the spirit world. This is a fundamental affirmation of the belief in life after death. Also, the evidence usually confirms that the loved one is okay on the other side. Whatever ailments or life trials suffered here on earth ended for them when they died. This one fact alone is vastly comforting to grievers. Additional evidence may indicate that the loved one is watching over the sitter, perhaps aware of upcoming events in their life. Knowing their loved one is still with them can soften the sitter's feelings of loss. There is comfort for them in knowing they are not as alone as they thought.

The actual message that the medium relays from the spirit is the most healing part of any reading. Regrets, guilt, and remorse over words spoken (or not) or actions taken (or not) can be eased by receiving a loving message from a loved one in spirit. I have watched many people receive messages that ran the gamut, from answering long-pondered questions to alleviating guilt to making them cry with relief at the information provided. Equally, it is very emotional to make contact with a deceased loved one and hear that they still love us. This alone can be healing. Having a deceased loved one send a message of love and support can remove some of the weight of grief. And sometimes, the delivery of the message can even involve physical sensations that cause the sitter to feel that the spirit of their loved one is actually present with them. That is truly healing.

The purpose of spiritual work is healing, in the broadest sense of the word. Spiritual healing knows no bounds in time or space. In other words, healing can go to the past, present, and future. And it can go to the other side of the veil. Even those in the spirit world may need healing, especially if they passed suddenly or with unresolved issues. So, it follows that healing is the most important part of mediumship.

Now, these different healing methods do not have to be practiced in isolation from one another. My sessions with Carolina included several components. There was always sound therapy and reiki. And as I sat for a while after receiving the treatment to ensure I was okay before I left, we would just talk. Sometimes we spoke as if she were a counselor, and other times, we discussed something about me that she picked up with her psychic abilities. Occasionally, she connected with my loved ones so they could give me a message. I never knew what services to expect before I showed up. All I knew was she kept the pain in my shoulder at bay, and I felt much better after every visit.

Healing can take many forms as long as we are open to it. There is a place for clinical medical advice or treatments. And there is also a place for the type of healing methods above. I typically exhausted traditional medical treatment methods before I searched for spiritual healings. But I have felt the benefits of direct healings to alleviate crushing stress. I have enjoyed the relief provided by energy healings. I cannot imagine how much more painful and onerous my grief journey would have been without direct and non-direct spiritual healings. For obvious reasons, I keep coming back to spiritual healing.

5. IT'S ALWAYS THERE

On the aircraft, there was much to enjoy about seat 1A. In the early eighties, a seat in first class gave the occupant the privilege of boarding last and exiting first. There was no need to sit as other passengers walked by and shot curious looks at you. You knew you could get whatever you wanted, from full dinner service with a selection of fine wines to blankets and pillows—choices designed with your comfort in mind. But the seat also allowed for minimum interruptions, if you so desired.

The fact is, I would rather not have been on the plane at all. I would have preferred that my father had not just died 4,400 miles away. I dreaded that I was flying to meet my mother. I would rather have been anywhere but in seat 1A. But there I was, with an elegant stewardess on high alert and casting concerned glances in my direction. She needed not to have worried. I have never been prone to public displays of any emotions. So, I was certain—well, as certain as I could be in my broken state—that I could hold myself together for the five-hour flight without disrupting the other passengers. I was well-practiced at the British "stiff upper lip" persona. So I sank into the large white leather seat, folded into myself, and leaned on the window as I tried desperately to keep my grief from killing me. A fancy cheese plate served on fine china and some tea sat on a small table beside me, all untouched. I clutched the crisp linen napkin in a death grip as I whimpered internally into my being, and silent tears drifted down my face. But I was holding it together.

At some point in the flight, I felt an incredible pull to look behind me. As I peeked between the seats, I saw a man sitting two rows back looking at me. Having seen him on local television, I immediately recognized him as a popular medium in my city. To say that I silently beseeched him to come and talk to me is an understatement. I used all my unbeknownst-to-me psychic powers to will him to come and help me. Steven rose from his seat and came over to me.

"May I join you?" he asked.

"Please," I replied.

He had barely sat down when he started to talk.

"He didn't feel a thing," he said. "And you know, he would have had brain damage if he had lived, and he would not have wanted that. He wants you to know that Willie came for him. And he brought a liver and white springer spaniel dog with him."

I had no reply. Five days prior, on the morning my father was to return home from a visit to Scotland, he had stepped out of bed and crumpled to the floor, dead from an unexpected heart attack. Finding out that his old hunting buddy, his uncle Willie, had come to meet him as he passed over, with a bird dog in tow, no less, was immensely comforting to me. I briefly wondered if my father had greeted the dog as "Sir" the way he always did with his dogs on the earth plane. I made a mental note to frame my picture of the three of them when I returned home.

Then Steven gestured to the cheese plate.

"Why don't you just grab a wedge of cheese from that plate and eat it as your dad would have?" he said.

I actually laughed. For in my mind's eye, I immediately replayed how my father would walk by the refrigerator, open the door, grab the cheese, cut a hunk of it off, and take a bite without breaking stride as he moved through the kitchen.

Steven and I talked about many things long since forgotten. Still, as he returned to his seat, I realized I had stopped weeping. The heaviness was gone. I no longer felt like I was dying. A calmness had enveloped me. I felt better, more peaceful. And I noticed that as Steven left the aircraft, the stewardess gave him a tote bag containing several bottles of wine. And she thanked him for taking care of the girl in seat 1A.

The thing about growing up is that in the day-to-day process, we often don't even notice the beliefs, values, habits, and traditions we accept and internalize. We simply absorb them effortlessly into the fabric of our being. They are familiar and known; there are no surprises. This makes them comfortable for us to return to them either by reflex or choice. And they stay with us whether we pay attention to them or not. It is not until we take a closer look at ourselves that we can determine what impact they have on our lives. And then, we can make the conscious choice to either embrace or discard them as we see fit. This was definitely the case with me.

Although the members of my mother's immediate family immigrated to Canada, without exception, they all left their hearts in Scotland. They came here to pursue a better economic life. Still, their heritage and upbringing were never part of the price to be paid for such an opportunity. The focus was always "back home." I cannot recall the number of times I heard statements like "It was never like this back home," or "Well, back home they . . ." And as the years passed, the most common refrain was "We need to go back home again this year."

A cursory glance at our home revealed a myriad of clues indicating that we led our lives in accordance with the shape of life in

Scotland. Visitors to the house could not help but notice the plaid clan crest and Robbie Burns plate proudly displayed on the walls or the thistle-patterned teacups laid out for tea. Anyone with an eye for detail could pick up on the authenticity of my kilts or the collection of silver kilt pins from the Isle of Skye, a Celtic cross, a Viking ship, swords, and grouse claws. The less visible habits were more telling. The record collection contained albums of bagpipe music. Hardly worn dresses were shipped back to the "old country" for a multitude of young cousins to get wear from. A local Scottish newspaper arrived weekly like clockwork from an aunt. The family swimming pool was kept at a brisk sixty-eight degrees Fahrenheit because that temperature reminded my father of his beloved North Sea.

Some rituals were strictly observed. Christmas Day was deemed as being specifically for children. Every effort was made to make it memorable for them. New Year's Eve was designated as a night only for adults. And on each of those evenings, the midnight toast was not made at midnight, but rather it was done at seven o'clock in the evening. The five-hour difference between Canada and their true home meant it was midnight in Scotland. These traditions were kept close and were always a priority. They were my heritage just as much as the checking of tea leaves after a cuppa and having a mother who spoke with those who had died.

People are relatively similar the world over when choosing their friends or community. They tend to gravitate to the comfort of the familiar. In other words, they select like-minded people similar to themselves. This is particularly true of immigrants. The Scots were no different. When my family moved to Canada, they socialized with other Scots. This was particularly necessary if one wanted to find the best Scottish bakery nearby.

My mother took this a step further. She always knew where to find the nearest Spiritualist church. She always seemed to come across the newest medium in town. She occasionally went out in the evening and came home to relate spiritual matters to my father. She clearly attended the odd spiritual meeting. I did not pay attention as I was busy leading my own life. However, upon reflection, it was evident that she found like-minded people with whom she shared interests because she sought them out. She did not leave meeting these folks to chance. She brought her Spiritualist practices to Canada and continued to practice her beliefs here. I can still see the routine when relatives came to Canada for a visit. The very first thing they all did was gather around the kitchen table with cups of tea. As soon as the first cup was drained dry, the reading of the tea leaves commenced. It was as routine as someone saying, "Pass me a biscuit, please."

Not surprisingly, the ritual of most importance was tea. My wee Scottish mum always had a pot of tea on the stove. Not a teabag in a cup, nor loose tea in a China teapot under some lovely tea cozy, but rather, she used a metal pot. That pot sat on the lowest burner setting, keeping the contents hot until just before the stage when a spoon might stand up in it unaided. And, of course, occasionally, when a bag broke, she would take a moment to look at the loose leaves in her cup to see what she could see.

I learned to drink it as a child when it was more milk and sugar than tea. And I kept adding milk and sugar to it as an adult. Far be it from me to deviate from the traditions of my Highland ancestors. But then came David, from a family that never drank tea. He was prepared to give it a whirl. That may have been because it was what was offered. Or perhaps he was being polite. More likely, it was because tea was never served without something to eat, and he needed something to wash down the accompanying snack.

However, he did not add sugar. My mother immediately but kindly labeled him a Lowlander. He kept that title for her entire life. And I spent the rest of his life trying to keep straight which cup was his when I served tea. If I am generous, I got it right maybe fifty percent of the time. The times I was correct were silent victories, so I don't recall them. But the times when he would take a sip and then say, "Ugh . . . this has sugar in it," or "Sweetie, this one is yours," well, I recall an awful lot of those.

No situation was too dire or celebratory that tea was not called for. And old habits die hard. This is particularly true when we don't even realize the automatic reflex until the moment has passed. I was at my cousin's house when her dad called from Scotland to say that her mother had been diagnosed with dementia. I immediately made tea; no thought, just reaction. We drank it as we considered what to do next because, well, that is what we both had been raised to do.

Similarly, after the police officers who came to notify me of David's death had departed, I made myself a cup of tea. I caught myself thinking that I had never even offered them one. Old habits do indeed die hard, even when someone has just died.

Being the only Canadian-born family member, it was a rootless upbringing for me. I was not from Scotland, but there was little opportunity provided to grow an attachment to the country of my birth. I felt like a semi-Scottish ex-pat who happened to be living in Canada. I lived in two worlds, each on opposite sides of an ocean. It was not dissimilar to the other type of living in two worlds in my house, each on opposite sides of the veil.

Additionally, I moved a lot in my life, never allowing for roots to grow in any one house, city, or country. None of the structures I resided in ever mattered much to me. I kept them nice and comfortable but never felt attached to the physical enclosures. They were simply places where I lived. I moved on with great ease from each one in turn.

Similarly, I have had little regard for the material things I have owned throughout my life. When I was nineteen, there was a fire in our house. My bedroom was gutted. Everything I possessed was gone except for the clothes I was wearing that day and a black turtleneck sweater a friend had borrowed. It was a huge lesson on the impermanence of the things we surround ourselves with in life. From that moment on, I never consciously formed attachments to possessions. I often said I collected only those things "that breathe." Fish, birds, cats, dogs, and friends took up residence in my homes over the years. I never tired of the sound of life throughout the house. I have always been tethered to people, not places. Home for me was the people in my life. From the time I met David, he was my home.

No one in my family adopted or even introduced any Canadian traditions. Indeed, it wasn't until I met David, an eighth-generation Canadian, that I fully realized that Canadians even had their own practices. David came from a farm family whose homestead was so established that its road reflected the family name. He was grounded to Canada not just by lineage and birth but also to the very earth of it. He spent his childhood summers at a cottage and winters playing hockey. But even as he introduced me to Canadian ways, I still retained my Scottish ways of living. I served goose instead of turkey for Christmas dinner. Dessert was a trifle (not pies) and real shortbread (not cookies). To this day, I still toast the arrival of Christmas and the New Year at seven o'clock.

On the spiritual side of life, my Scottish traditions remained equally strong. I made sure no one ever put new shoes on a table. I wore a kilt pin on the inside of my barrister's robes when I went to court to keep my father close. And I still clean my house on New Year's Eve to welcome the new year because doing otherwise would be bad luck. And although David never displayed much interest or belief in the more spiritual side of life, I still remember the day the flatbed truck came to take his motorcycle away after he died. Before the truck arrived, I got down on my knees in the garage and removed a copper spirit bell that he had attached to the bike's frame, a good luck charm purported to keep riders safe. When it comes to the spiritual side of life, nationality has no bearing.

I did not delve into or actively pursue any spiritual activities until after both of my parents had died. To this, I have often said to myself, "My bad!" However, I have given myself grace concerning these missed moments by recognizing that we only come to our spirituality when we are ready. We cannot force ourselves to hear. But when we are ready or in need, Spirit will step forward to help us by bringing the necessary people and opportunities into our lives.

As a teenager, I read popular books by Hesse, Bach, and Gibran. And I had no end of conversations with friends about the meaning and purpose of life here and beyond. However, after high school, I got busy living life. I always knew my spiritual heritage was there. It was just percolating under the surface, never static, always alive. Like the other experiences of my upbringing, I knew that it was an integral part of me, part of my soul's DNA. And I always believed that when my soul needed comfort, Spiritualists were the people I could rely on. More importantly, I knew they were who I needed to turn to for help and healing. Even though they may not have been at the top of my mind daily, they were brought forth into my life when dire circumstances occurred. I just needed to recognize them and reach out. That is what happened on that aircraft. That was spiritual healing at 35,000 feet.

However, I did not realize that communication between myself and the spirits on the other side was a two-way street. It did not only happen when I was hurting or instigated it. While I was busy just thinking of the spirits when it suited me, I did not consider that they might have been trying to talk to me too. It never occurred to me that they might try to warn me or shield me from impending tragedy. But they did.

After my mother died, she only came to me in my dreams (that I recall) three times. The first time occurred five years after her death. I do not recall the circumstances in the first dream except that my brother died suddenly and unexpectedly less than two weeks later. I remember at the time, I tied the dream to his death in the form of a warning, for he had also been in the dream.

Some seven years later, I dreamt of my mother again. This time she sat on the arm of a sofa with my dog Karma beside her. Karma was my little white spaniel who preferred hanging out in the garage with the boys to lying in the house on a soft bed. She favored the feel of the freshly churned vegetable patch dirt to that of the manicured grass. She was a pretty little thing who coasted through her fourteen years on earth solely on her looks and charm, but she had the heart of a farm dog. A week after the dream, my seemingly healthy pet started throwing up for no apparent reason. A rushed trip to her veterinarian turned into a race against time to get to the city's emergency veterinary services with test results in hand. There were more tests, x-rays, and an ultrasound. The afternoon turned to the evening, and the evening turned to nightfall. Then, there was a terminal diagnosis. There were no treatment options. The internist kept saying how sorry he was. I was shell-shocked and weeping.

"If she was my dog, I would do the kindest thing," he said. My heart shattered.

The third time my mother came in a dream was four months before David died. I dreamt I was being attacked by someone. I could not see who it was clearly, and I tried to scream for help. But no sound came out of my mouth. I could not make any noise to cry out. But I could see my mother standing in an open doorway just watching. I couldn't understand why she wasn't helping me. She was just watching. I woke up with a start, my heart pounding and a silent scream stuck in my throat. But I put the memory of that dream in the recesses of my mind because the only person in it was me. But it was a warning, and the signs from the other side continued to come.

When David and I lived in Vancouver, my parents came to visit us. We showed them around the city, took a ferry to Victoria, and then drove up the Icefields Parkway through the Rocky Mountains to Jasper National Park. One evening while we were walking to a restaurant for dinner, David and I were trailing about twenty feet behind my parents. Suddenly, David slowed and turned to look at me. He looked so serious.

"Sweetie, I don't mean to alarm you, but he's done," he said.

I looked at my father. I knew he had had some minor strokes a couple of years prior, but he had been given the all-clear after surgery. But as I looked at him through the lens of David's comment, I understood what he was saying. My father's gait was slightly less sure than usual. He seemed bone-weary or maybe soul-tired. It was as if living required a special effort on his part. It wasn't the expected effects of aging but something I could not quite put my finger on. But I could feel it; something terrible was coming. And it did when he died suddenly within the following year. The other side had been showing me, but when I did not get the message, they used David to step in to tell me.

Several weeks before David died, he puttered about in his garage, and I sat in a lawn chair chatting to him. At one point, he went out into the driveway to retrieve something. And that's when I saw it. Looking at the back of David as he walked away, I saw my father all those years ago on the street in Jasper.

He's done, I thought.

I had the distinct impression he was moving towards the veil. This time, I didn't need anyone to point anything out or clarify the message. I simply sat there shocked and tried to make sense of the feeling in the pit of my stomach. I never mentioned it to David. I felt like it was a secret between the universe and me. However, I also felt like I had just boarded a train, one that was hurtling down the tracks to a destination I did not want to arrive at. But I didn't know how to get off the train.

The day David died was a warm summer day. I sat in the living room as he packed his motorcycle with some extra clothes for an overnight ride to another city. He came in and asked me to do up the bottom of his chaps. Then he leaned over the couch to kiss my cheek before leaving. He said, "I love you," and headed for the door. How many times had we done that? I don't know except to say "many." But that day, a feeling in my soul made me get off the sofa to go out and see him off. It was not dread, but it was a powerful feeling that I could not deny.

As I stood there hugging him, I remembered a meme I had seen online about how the things that matter over our lives together are not the material things we acquire but rather that we have one another. I told him this and how much I had always loved him and more. And he told me the same. A summing up of a lifetime in love, if you will. And then he drove off, never to return.

I will always be grateful for the push from the spirit world I received that day. It made me get up off the sofa and tell him once more precisely how much he always had and still meant to me. Also, it allowed him to tell me the same. For in situations where death is unexpected and sudden, as David's was later that day, we do not usually think to take the time or opportunity to say the things we would choose to say if we had a warning. I was afforded a warning. However, it was not presented in a negative framework. The feeling of going outside to him had no sense of foreboding to it. I never felt like this would be my last chance to say these things to him. It was as if I just wanted to express them in a context of love as opposed to one of goodbye. Despite the dreams and realizations of the previous few months, I never realized that he would not be home the next day. I believe the force that pulled me outside to say these things gave me the option to have no regrets in this regard. In essence, I was given a chance to protect myself going forward by making my impending grief journey a little less onerous. The burden of grief is heavy enough without the added weight of regrets and words left unsaid.

When David died, we lived in a small beach town. The house was at the end of a cul-de-sac. No one drove onto the street unless they lived there or were lost. So when I saw the police cars silently creeping along the road with their flashing lights piercing the darkness, I knew. I knew in my heart that they were coming to our house, and I knew what they would say. I am not sure how I knew. It may have been that my conscious, rational mind put the pieces together and, by chance, jumped to the correct conclusion. Or it may have been that my unconscious mind scanned the plethora of signs I had experienced and landed on the most probable outcome. Or maybe my intuition kicked in and what I knew in my soul to be true was suddenly also something that I knew in my being to be true.

When the police officers and trauma workers left, I slowly detached from everything I had previously known. I started to experience a surreal sense of pieces of myself letting go of each other and, more importantly, letting go of whatever remained of me tethered to the earth. David was gone. And just like when he had left to finish his apprenticeship or went away on business, I became unmoored. Those departures had been minor in the true scope of life. However, I had been under intense stress at those times in my life, which had made his absences unbearable. This was different. I hadn't been under any pressure, but the loss was permanent this time. My true north was gone forever. This time, my entire foundation gave way. This was unlike any death in my life before it, and there had been many. There was no psychiatrist nor tranquilizers to soften this. Nothing could ease this. This was worse. This was way worse. I had no idea what to expect. And I was terrified.

Grief came like an avalanche. I was paralyzed, unable to escape it as it thundered down upon me. I watched it slowly crash over me. It took the feet from under me and the very breath from my lungs.

And then the silence engulfed me as I thought about how to save myself from suffocating from the weight of it. An incredible sense of weightlessness entered my consciousness. Time became some amorphous concept that started to distort and slow down. I heard nothing and felt even less. I couldn't process any thoughts effectively. I felt utterly disoriented as if I was operating on a different level in another world. Grief had taken hold.

It took a long time before grief and I came to an understanding. First, I had to suffer. Then I did what I always did when I needed comforting, I found my way to the Spiritualists. For they are the true believers who are experienced in spiritual healing. Spiritualism is their religion and their culture. There was no denying it; it was also mine. I started the long journey home to my heritage and my spiritual roots.

6. DARK NIGHT
OF THE SOUL

In the latter half of the sixteenth century, a Spanish mystic, John of the Cross, was a member of the Carmelite religious order. His efforts to reform the order led to his imprisonment. During that time, he penned a poem called "The Dark Night of the Soul," which was, in essence, a spiritual odyssey. It recounts the soul's journey from its bodily home to its union with God. John's writings set out the symptoms and stages of this experience.

The most crucial first symptom of a Dark Night of the Soul experience is the experiencing of extreme pain, a period of deep, deep despair. Then life takes on the appearance of being meaningless, which leads to asking questions and seeking answers. Pondering the more profound aspects of life and a study of spiritual practices around the world leads to the sufferer resonating with one or more spiritual philosophies. A path is revealed; a life's purpose found. John believed that quieting the mind (meditating) would lead to discovering one's life purpose and, perhaps, reveal an inner capacity for healing. The final stage is meeting one's soul tribe and eventual spiritual awakening.

Today, the phrase "Dark Night of the Soul" is often used casually to describe a challenging and painful period in one's life, for example, after the death of a loved one, the break-up of a marriage, or the diagnosis of a life-threatening illness. There is nothing wrong with this informal usage. Still, it differs significantly from the original meaning and context of the phrase, as first conceived by the Spanish priest. The loneliness, isolation, and fear spawned by the recent global pandemic was a glimpse into the beginning of such an experience for many. However, few people who claim to have had a Dark Night of the Soul experience progress past the first stage or experience much past the first few symptoms.

The reality is that virtually no one goes through the Dark Night itself, which is in actuality the soul's journey to unite with God. Instead, in most cases, the soul goes through a transition and ultimately embarks on a spiritual journey that rarely, if ever, reaches the final stage as envisioned by John. But this experience can be a lifesaver even in its shortened versions. It can provide answers to life, kick-start spiritual journeys, and lead to meditation and mindful living. Indeed, that is how it was for me.

How I dealt with each death throughout my life was different. After my uncle died, I fled out west to live. Running and keeping busy are avoidance tactics familiar to many grievers. When my father died several years later, I went to work during the day and did cocaine by night for weeks. I was "a mess," as my best friend so eloquently put it. Eventually, David gently put his foot down, and I pulled myself together. I put on a brave face to be strong for David when his father died. The unexpected deaths of my mother and her sister on the same day several years later decimated me. I sat at the kitchen table for two months, simply crying. I could not function until one day when I decided I could and returned to work.

When my brother died a few years later, I had no tears for him until two years after his death, and even then, they were tears of frustration from having to sort out his estate. It wasn't that I didn't love him. I was just done. I was in survival mode. Without realizing it, I had reacted to each death just as I had seen my family do. I pushed the pain down, compartmentalized the grief, and kept moving. There was no introspection, no seeking of answers, no spiritual journey. There was never a step beyond the first symptom of the Dark Night of the Soul experience. But then David died. Nothing in my life had prepared me for the crushing heaviness of loss where his absence filled every molecule of my being. No one warned me about the journey. I entered very unfamiliar territory.

About six months after David died, I realized nobody was coming to save me. Indeed, it was crystal clear to me by then that no one else could save me. That was my job. And I made the conscious decision to double down on saving myself. Several people in the grief support group I attended (without fail, I might add) had mentioned several upcoming blue Christmas services. These are special seasonal services designed for grievers. So I went in search of such a gathering. And that's when I saw the advertisement. A night of "Music and Messages" was going to be presented by a local Spiritualist church. And that was all it took. I was in. No one was left on this side of the veil to help me. I needed to find a way for them to help me from where they were.

When I arrived, I felt more than just a little nervous as I crossed the parking lot in the icy air. My outside self was bundled up in a parka, scarf, and gloves, but none of it was enough to warm even the edges of my frozen soul. My inside self was inconsolably bereft, awash in a heavy, dense sadness accompanied by a sense of not being attached to the earth in any meaningful way. I steeled myself to perform the rudimentary actions at the check-in table in a manner that would not attract any unwanted attention. I gathered all of my remaining energy to turn to look into the church. And at the precise moment I turned, my entire being was enveloped and absorbed by a soft warmth. I was drawn into the candlelit pews as if by an unseen force. Such a sense of peace and welcoming overcame me that I almost floated to my seat. I felt like I was home. I felt, for the first time since David had died, that I might be able to heal from the trauma of his passing.

The music was uplifting, and the presentation of the program was professional, even though it had the feeling of being at the home of a loving family. I watched with interest as the mediums delivered messages to attendees between the songs. They were dispensing so much empathy, compassion, and comfort. And then suddenly, with little warning, I was chosen to be the next recipient of a healing message. The medium had been pacing slowly around the altar, giving the evidence of the spirit with her. I recognized that she had connected to my father. And she realized it too. It seemed to take only an instant for her to identify me as the person he was there to speak to. She stopped and looked at me directly.

"May I work with you?" she asked gently.

I nodded.

"I have your father with me," she said.

She offered up accurate details of his passing. She mentioned how he fancied himself an outstanding dancer, particularly in his youth, confirming that he had met my mother at a dance. She discussed how he was an animal lover, particularly noting how much he loved dogs. She described the dog that was with him in spirit in detail. (It was the last dog he owned on this earth.) Then, she offered evidence that he was watching me. She mentioned that he liked my new car and thought it was a nice, safe car for me.

"Once a dad, always a dad," she said with a smile. I felt relieved since my new car was the very first car I had ever purchased by myself or even owned in my entire life.

When she finished providing the evidence necessary to prove her connection and demonstrate that those who have passed are still with us and see what we are doing, she mentioned a couple of upcoming events in my life. She detailed a short trip I was preparing to take, saying it would be good for me. (It turned out it was.) She also brought up a friend saying she would have a tough Christmas and need support from me. (This came to pass when a friend lost her adored pet for over a week at Christmastime.) Finally, the reading ended with the message.

"Your father says you have had a lower vibration of late," she said. "You have to raise your vibration to make it easier for them to get to you, to help you. I see him behind you, wrapping you in a soft shawl. He is sprinkling a kind of fairy dust over you. He just wants to comfort you."

I had no idea what she was talking about. Raise my vibration? What vibration? Raise it how? But it didn't matter that I did not know what she meant. I could find out. For the first time in half a year, I felt calm enough to be able to find a direction to move in. I would just need to find someone who knew about such things and ask. Perhaps, just perhaps, I could pull myself out of the darkness that is known as grief.

All things in the universe are constantly vibrating. Humans are made up of particles of vibrating energy that comprise atoms that comprise a collection of cells. And the vibrational frequency level of a person can be measured just as the vibrational frequency level of, say, music or the earth can be determined. The theory is that spirits vibrate at a much higher frequency than humans. So, if spirits vibrate at a higher frequency, they must come down to our level to communicate with us. Guilt, anger, regret, and sadness are some of the emotions that can further reduce our normal frequency level, making it even harder for spirits to connect with us. We need to remove these barriers. We have to make it easier for them to communicate with us by opening our hearts and raising our vibration. This can be done by chanting, singing, praying, and meditating. We have all felt the effects of raised vibrations. It is the feeling we experience when the crowd cheers at a sporting event or sings along at a concert, or when a congregation recites a prayer out loud in unison.

I chose meditation as the way I would attempt to raise my vibration. One purpose of meditation is to quiet the mind. Another is to achieve a mentally clear and emotionally calm state. It is also practiced in numerous religious traditions to reach a heightened spiritual awareness. All of these goals sounded good to me. However, I had never meditated in my life. I had to start at the beginning, just focusing on something in an effort to calm down.

I considered this for a couple of months after the medium from the church had raised the issue of my low vibration. Then, one day, I recalled that the wife of one of David's friends practiced reiki. She would know, I thought. I booked a reiki treatment with her. Although I had moved back to town only three months before, I had lived here for fifteen years in a long-ago part of my life and had visited often during the intervening years. I had no trouble finding her office. Her office space was exactly as I expected: a narrow but deep first-floor storefront location with a yoga studio at the front and a private treatment room at the back. When I entered, she got up from the little cafe table she had been sitting at.

"Hi, Diane. I was sorry to hear about David," she said.

I nodded. Ah yes, I thought. I had forgotten how nothing escapes the grapevine in towns where everyone knows everyone else.

She performed the reiki treatment, similar to the treatments I remembered getting a decade before, complete with the singing bowl first step. It centered me to a place of tranquility in a nanosecond. After the treatment, I asked her about meditating as a way to increase my vibration.

"Why don't you start with a short Kundalini meditation?" she said. "The repetition of a mantra releases the energy in the body upward."

"Okay," I said, wondering what she was talking about.

She gave me a short tutorial. She showed me where to find the link to a recording online. Then she went through it with me. It was only twelve minutes. She demonstrated how to use the thumbs of each hand to touch each of the fingers on the same hand while reciting "Sa-Ta-Na-Ma." The words were spoken for two minutes, whispered for two minutes, said in the mind for four minutes, whispered again for two minutes, and finally spoken for the last two minutes. Done. Perfect, I thought. I could handle this. And every night for the next four months, I recited Sa-Ta-Na-Ma, Sa-Ta-Na-Ma, Sa-Ta-Na-Ma, over and over and over for twelve minutes, just before I went to sleep. It felt good to accomplish even this. Then I fell asleep listening to Tibetan sound therapy recordings of singing bowls and bells. My anxiety lessened, if only just for the time before bedtime. It was a start.

In the meantime, the passage of time and the grief work I was doing led to an easing of the sadness. And I was seeking information. I devoured books by Dyer, Tolle, Zukav, and others. I learned about Eastern mysticism, the intricacies of the soul, and how to be more in tune with myself and the universe. I had always been a glass-half-full girl, but I made a more concerted effort to keep negativity out of my life. My outlook had started to change for the better.

I started to move towards giving up control of the things I had no control of and trusting that things would unfold as they were meant to. Most importantly, I focused on being kind. It's not that I was not a kind person before, but this was different. This was a focus and a goal. There is always room for improvement in this area. But as I watched the news, read a comment online, or listened to someone complain about someone, my thought was always the same.

"Just be kind."

This approach was a step beyond how I had lived my life before David's death. I recall many times in my professional life when I would react to someone by noting that they did not need to be mean. But not being mean is not the same thing as being kind. Not being mean simply means the person adopts a neutral stance. They are not being mean but nor are they being kind. Being kind means they need to take their action up a couple of notches and actually add something positive to the world. As I expanded my thoughts this way, I also wanted to expand my knowledge of meditation. It seemed to me that clear thinking needed a calm, focused mind. It was the logical next step.

Meditation is a stilling of the mind. I had never mastered it. I had trouble keeping errant thoughts from racing through my mind. As I tried to empty my mind, my grocery list, pending errands, or other minutiae rushed in to fill the void. On the other hand, a guided meditation is a stilling of the mind resulting from listening to a guiding voice. Even with a guided meditation, while I tried to focus on the guide's voice, my mind wandered, but the guide's voice would bring me back. I have always preferred this second method.

When I felt ready to take the next step up from my twelve-minute rote meditation, I sought out an open circle group. In the context of Spiritualism, an open circle group is a group of people who come together on a drop-in basis to enjoy the space and connect with Spirit. It provides a safe, supportive, and respectful place for people to experience a group meditation journey under the direction of a practicing medium. The participants can meditate and develop their psychic and mediumship skills in a group setting. Privacy is paramount, and no one is obligated to reveal anything they see, hear, or feel in their own personal meditation. However, the group is available for discussion and guidance concerning anything offered for discussion on a strictly confidential basis. The class I attended allotted thirty minutes for each meditation and discussion portion, so it was a one-hour commitment each week. This circle met in Scotland, but when Covid lockdowns came, the circle moved online seamlessly. The new format had no impact on the actual effects of the meditation.

The mediums that ran the circle I attended were exceptionally gifted. While leading the guided meditation, they also tuned into every person in the class. When the meditation was over, and people were discussing their experiences, the mediums could mention circumstances that related to certain people. For example, they may have noticed someone experiencing pain and sent healing at the time. Or, they may have also seen some of the actual images a person saw. More than once, the mediums picked up on the spirits working with various people during the meditation. They did this by seeing, hearing, or feeling them.

All meditations, whether done alone or in a group, have the same essential elements; breathe, quiet the mind, and allow the energy to build. Only the methods to achieve this goal differ. In Spiritualist circles, there is a final step; we invite spirits from the other side of the veil to blend with us. Whereas prayers are talking to God, meditation is listening for guidance.

The first meditations in the open circle group were very simple. One of the most popular ones involved picturing a white flame in the chest. On each inhale, the flame got brighter, and on each exhale, it got bigger. Eventually, the flame was expanded throughout the entire body and then outside of the body. Variations on the meditation had the flame expanding to the room, the group, or the world. As easy as this may sound, the first meditations were very hard for me. My mind was still racing, and unimportant thoughts were still trying to take up space in my mind. I certainly did not relax as I was supposed to. It was, to my mind, an awful lot like work. Plus, I had a lot of questions. Like how does one expand energy? Is it visualization, or do we feel it? Is it some combination of the two? Do we will it to happen, or does it happen just because we ask for it to happen? I am still not sure of the answers to those questions. But with practice, I got better at it. At first, I just wanted to last through the class without my mind taking too many detours. Before long, I not only managed to stay with the entire meditation, but I actually felt relaxed afterward.

My first meditations revealed many different things I could see and hear in my mind during the meditation. The only person in the group surprised by this was me. My most common first reaction was that I saw swaths of indigo and purple, both colors associated with the third eye. Then I would see a sage green color (associated with the heart) move within the purple or indigo. I learned that seeing colors while meditating is widespread. As time went on, I started to see things I recognized for what they were, such as eyes or sets of lips. I learned that this, too, was very common. I also learned that an increase in visuals means increased spiritual development.

In the beginning, I saw blazing suns and a lot of hearts, an awful lot of hearts of all sizes and colors. Occasionally I would see the entire face of someone, but it was never anyone I knew. It wasn't very long before I could see little scenes or vignettes in my mind's eye. They would play out like a scene in a movie. One day, I saw a wolf as it stood at the top of a mountain overlooking a valley. On other days I watched as a man embraced a woman or gave her a kiss, but again, the people were unrecognizable to me. I also heard things being said in my mind. But they didn't sound any different from the occasional things I heard spoken in my mind, in my conscious daily life.

"I love you."

"I miss you."

These were the phrases I heard most often, but who was saying these things to me was a mystery. Someone loved me. Someone missed me. But since my entire family, except for my son, is on the other side, it could have been any of several people. The biggest mystery to me has been that from the very beginning of my meditations, I have often heard the name Michael being said to me while I meditate. I have no idea why or what it means, as it is not the name of anyone in my family or a name that is significant to me in any way. It is something I am confident I will understand when the time is right for me to do so.

As my meditating skills improved, I started to feel the experience. Feeling is critical to knowing that Spirit is drawing close. Sometimes, I felt energy swirling around me or had the feeling that someone was stroking my cheek or playing with my hair. I also had intense pain several times. The first time it happened, the pain started in my neck. It was constant, and at one point, it felt like how I imagined the feeling of being shot with a gun. All of this was on the left side of my neck, head, and shoulder. It was excruciating. When I came out of the meditation, the pain disappeared. The medium leading the circle came to me first. She had been watching me squirm with discomfort.

"When that happens," she said, "ask the spirits to step back and lower the pain. And if they do not, just come out of the meditation and then go back in."

One explanation for feeling physical pain when meditating is that it indicates our inability to blend with the spirit. This happens because we are not used to it. It takes time for us to learn to adjust. Another explanation is that the spirits are giving us the pain of someone who had this issue, just mixing up their methods of communication. I also learned that feeling sensations during a meditation could include physically feeling emotions resulting from a heart connection. I could feel love being sent to me several times, warming my soul. Other times, I could feel overwhelming sadness such that I would emerge from the session with tears on my cheeks. Both emotions disappeared immediately upon exiting the meditation, just as the physical pain did.

A connection with a spirit during the meditation can be evident by a feeling of heat we experience as they come in. Equally, a sense of cold can come over us at the end of the meditation when they leave. It can be so cold that having a blanket nearby to cover our legs is advisable. Also, we must make sure that we return fully from any meditation. To that end, drinking water to ground ourselves is a good practice, as is making sure our feet are firmly on the floor.

In my first open circle meditation, I saw the colors purple and indigo in my mind's eye, but that was all. It was an auspicious start, I thought. I was assured it was a very common first step. The following week I visualized nothing at all in the session. It was a complete bust. However, in the third week, I got a glimpse of what I might be able to do. We were guided to a point in the meditation where we were to sit on a bench in a forest setting and spend about ten minutes in silence. I could see myself in my mind. I sat on a bench above a ravine where my husband and I had hiked. I looked down on the river and over the tops of the forest. A man walked along the path to me and sat down on the bench but did not touch me. I could not make out any discernible features concerning his face or clothes or see any other identifying hints. Still, I knew in my heart it was David.

"I am here," he said softly. The words were so clear in my head.

"You're not here," I said. Was there a tinge of petulance in my mental tone?

"I am here where it matters," he said. I took this to mean that he was on the other side where he was meant to be.

We sat together in silence and gazed over the trees. Coming out of the meditation, I saw the sage green color taking up my entire view. Still, a windshield wiper cleared it like it would clear snow from a car's front windshield. I felt the message was "It should clear, your view should clear."

Afterward, the others talked about what they heard and saw in their meditations and gave messages to one another. Suddenly, a woman said she had received three names of spirits that were present and were sending love. The names were John, William, and Betty. No one claimed this message. So I did. For these were the names of my father, father-in-law, and mother-in-law, all of whom are in spirit.

That particular open circle class was a pivotal experience for me. It showed me that, for starters, I could master the skill of quieting my mind. Additionally, it reinforced my belief that my family was around me, supporting my efforts. Most importantly, it demonstrated that I could talk to David in real-time, so to speak. And that fact alone was enough to make me try harder. I thought the work would be worth it if I could converse with him, albeit only in my mind.

Other meditations were highly complex. For example, I participated in one meditation where I listened intently as the medium took us on a journey. She guided us along a path, past mountains and rivers, to the edge of some water. There, a boat was waiting to take us to an island. On the island, we went into a house and asked for a drink of water. We then had to walk along at the base of stone walls into a room in a building. We were shown a book on a table. We returned by the same route. This particular meditation was designed to allow for a timeline. It allowed us to put things in places and structure the process. It also indicated where our thoughts would go; for example, to each other, collective consciousness, our guides, Spirit, and so on.

When I did this meditation, I actually recalled very little of it. Unbeknownst to me at the time, this journey was to the Isle of Iona, a very spiritual place in Scotland. When one goes to the Isle of Iona, one goes by boat. The guide referred to the first building as a house, but it was actually a former nunnery. Next were the ruins of an abbey. I could not remember anything after the nunnery. But I remembered it very clearly. About five or six women were in it, all dressed in 1700s-style garb. I could see rudimentary furniture from that era in there as well. But I did not remember going to, being inside, or returning from the abbey.

In fact, at one point, my head snapped back, and I was brought back into the meditation from somewhere else. There are various theories as to what occurs when this happens. The most straightforward explanation is that one falls asleep. I know I did not fall asleep. Instead, the snap of my head was spirits calling me back. They may have been working on me on a deeper level with healing or perhaps were imparting information to me. Or maybe I went too deep into a trance meditation where they could not work with me effectively. In any event, back I came.

Meditating is also known as "sitting in the power." It is called this when we are sitting in the power of Spirit, the Source, oneness, all that is, and so on. Sitting in the power is being aware of ourselves as a soul. It is remembering who we are and feeling into our soul. It is the meditating we do when preparing to work and develop our skills. We are attuning to Spirit to receive healing, shared knowledge, and teachings as Spirit sees fit. I trust that I will be shown what it is that I need to learn to make my journey more complete. So, to that end, I now start each meditation with an intent. I repeat it silently to myself.

"Show me what I need to know and tell me what I need to hear." And then I wait to see what happens.

Our rational minds may never understand what has happened, but if we can keep them open, our hearts will find their own intuitive way. And that is what I wished for myself as I embarked on a spiritual journey following the path set out by a Spanish mystic all those years ago. I needed to heal myself. I needed to drag myself out of the quagmire of despair and find a new path. But for the first time since David had died, I felt like I could see glimpses of the road. I was going home. I was going home to my soul. And there were others on both sides of the veil to help me.

7. THEY WALK WITH ME

One of my greatest fears as a young woman was being awakened in the night by an intruder and being the victim of an assault in my home. Still, this fear did not propel me to take any self-defense classes or martial arts training. As we Canadians are not allowed to have guns, I knew that in the unlikely occurrence of such an event, it would come down to me and my wits. And I often wondered what I would do if the situation did present itself. I always thought I would freeze, panic, and be unable to think clearly enough to defend myself. As self-assured as I was in my everyday life, I could not picture myself fighting back and having the upper hand against an assailant in the dead of night in a darkened room. I discovered that my imaginings about this scenario were nowhere near accurate.

In the early eighties, David and I lived on the main floor of a house, with others renting the basement and second-floor apartments. From a safety perspective, it seemed sufficient with its solid doors, locks that worked, and other renters within earshot. It was a typical pattern in our neighborhood. We were close enough to downtown, bordering on decidedly sketchy areas but far enough removed to be close to where families were more common. When David went out of province for a week, I wasn't afraid; not at the beginning, not in the middle, not until the end.

I was alone, asleep at two in the morning, and I awoke to hear someone fussing with the front door lock. By the time I realized what the sound was, it had stopped. Had the person left? In a momentary grasp for comfort, I clutched the duvet to my neck as I thought about what to do next. Suddenly, people entered through the back door. I listened to the inaudible sounds of muffled whispers between two men. Still, I was hyperventilating, and the sound of my own gasps drowned out their voices. My heart raced as adrenalin surged through my body, and there was a deafening pounding in my ears. I just could not hear clearly! The trauma from realizing that my worst fear was coming true started to set in.

I decided to lie still, pretend to be asleep, and then run for it when the door was unobstructed. Maybe it was not the best escape plan, but it was a plan. I was still trying to formulate it when one of the men left almost as quickly as the two had entered. I had been waiting for my path to the door to be clear when the remaining man entered the bedroom. Trying to focus through barely opened eyes, I lay motionless in the dark. I pretended to be asleep as I watched the man stop at my dresser briefly and then proceed to David's dresser. He rummaged around on the dresser. Then the man started to undo his belt. And I was done play-acting. I went straight up the wall and leaped off the bed, bolting for the exit.

"Diane!" he yelled. And ever the athlete, David grabbed me as I reached the door.

I never slept that night. David just held me while I shook for most of it. The fear had been one thing. And the trauma had been quite another. David never entered our home for the remaining decades of our lives together without calling out to me from the door. But what shocked me to my core was how lucid my mind had been. I knew I would have shot this man dead if I had had access to a gun; no warnings, no questions, no qualms. That was quite a revelation for a hippie girl. It turned out that I was not entirely the girl I had thought I was. Clearly, I was made of much sterner stuff.

I have never forgotten that night, nor the things I learned. Most importantly, I discovered that things rarely play out as we imagine they might. It is hard to have control of a situation when you may not be able to see the entire picture. And others are operating from within their perceptions of reality. David had unexpectedly come home a day early. Hence, he was creeping around, being quiet as he dispatched the cab driver. He had expected I would be sleeping and took my hyperventilating for snoring. But I discovered that even when I have a skewed version of reality, I can act within my version of events to save myself. I realized that I can be traumatized and still function. Indeed, I can think very clearly. I can choose when and how to act. I learned that I have a pretty strong sense of survival at my core.

People have parroted sentiments of how strong I have become since David died. Personally, I don't put any stock in those claims. I didn't need his death to make me stronger. And I am not any stronger than I was before he died. The truth is, even on a good day, I am often still entirely broken inside. But I have always been strong. The events of that night in Vancouver drove that message home to me. And there were several incidents in my past where this was apparent to others. I can still see my mother-in-law move to my side as we stood at my own mother's grave site, to whisper in my ear.

"You can do this," she said. "You are the strongest woman I know."

I wasn't convinced. As it happened, my mother and aunt had died one hundred miles apart, within three hours of one another. Both deaths were sudden and unexpected. I like to think my mother grabbed her sister's hand on the way to cross over; sisters in life and sisters in death. But I was pretty devastated by it all. There was no one left in the generations above me. And my aunt's funeral was two days after my mother's. When the bagpipes of a lone Scottish piper wailed as her casket came in, I thought I would finally break into a million pieces. But I could still hear the words "the strongest woman I know." And I held onto that. I still hold onto that to this day.

David's death rocked my world beyond anything imaginable. The thing was, I had always seen David as the stronger person in our relationship. I believed I leaned on him more than he ever leaned on me. Perhaps this is what happens when two strong, independent people come together. We don't notice ourselves relying on the other, nor do we ever feel leaned on by them. I wasn't sure I could survive his death, but he came through to confirm my strength. I found myself listening to several mediums give me messages from him that ran along the lines of:

"You were the strength of us. You gave me strength. I was strong because you were there beside me."

And, "David says he could not have done what you have done. He says he could not have coped without you."

And I knew, somehow, I could survive this loss. But I also knew I was getting a lot of help from the other side. My upbringing had taught me it was there, but I needed to figure out to recognize it, access it, and accept it. My bereavement may have looked like a journey of one to people on earth, but I knew a group effort was at play.

And so, the signs came fast and furious after his death. On the very first day, I suddenly heard the words "Buck up, buttercup" in my head as I laced up my boots in preparation for taking his dog for a walk. I knew it was David. It wasn't that it sounded like his voice, but I had never heard anyone else ever say that phrase. He was telling me not to weaken. As I walked the beach for weeks afterward, it was awash with thousands of butterflies, the result of a Monarch butterfly migration that I learned was a highly unusual occurrence in the area. I found dimes everywhere they should not have been. Lights flickered, and doors were opened. And then, one day, my son called. He told me he had a picture of his dad and himself sitting on a bookshelf. It would be facing one direction in the morning but turned 180 degrees to face the opposite direction when he got home at night. I told him to just ask his dad to stop moving it. I had done this when I came home a couple of times, and the basement door was open. The fact is, it scared me, so I asked David not to do that. It never happened again.

About eighteen months after his death, I sat with a medium who listed all the signs I had been getting without me telling her a thing.

"David is very tactile. He turns your son's picture around. He sends dimes and feathers, the physical things. He also sends you warm fuzzies," she said. That was an interesting turn of phrase, I thought. I recalled a book about warm fuzzies that David and I had read the first year we had dated and had continually referenced throughout our lives together. It still sits on my bookshelf today. But the medium continued speaking.

"Your mother, on the other hand, sends the softer things, like the butterflies, all different kinds and colors," she said. "She also sends you scents. And you can hear her." I wondered if it was my mother speaking to me when I occasionally awoke in the morning to hear someone calling my name as if they were in the next room. And I marveled at how I was sometimes overwhelmed with the scent of perfume. The fact is, I have had no sense of smell for several decades. Still, when the perfume scent suddenly comes on so strong that sometimes I can even taste it, I am reminded that I am not alone.

But the sign that stopped me in my tracks was the fireflies. One evening, a week after David had died, I sat on a friend's porch discussing selling David's truck when, suddenly, I noticed a swarm of fireflies on her lawn. It was the first time I had ever seen them in my life. I was mesmerized. I also felt he was telling me it was okay to sell his truck. It was pretty comforting. The following weekend I was on her porch again as I was handing his truck over the next day. The fireflies were back. One firefly flew up to my face and just hovered there. It was so close that I could see the firelight pulsating in its tail.

For several minutes, time was suspended, and it felt like that firefly and I were the only two living things in the world. I was not alone. I sold his truck the next day without any qualms.

The most prolific sign I received after he died was a ringing in my ears. It is thought that the ringing in one's ears is actually the tearing of the veil to the other side. Someone is coming through to console us and let us know they are there. Ringing in the right ear is believed to be masculine energy coming through. Ringing in the left ear is believed to be feminine energy. According to my journals, I had fifty-six incidents of ringing in my right ear and eighty-five in my left. They sounded like a shrill whistle, a bell chime, a drumbeat, humming, and thumping. They have been faint or loud and lasted varying amounts of time, usually under ten seconds. But what they all had in common was a silence that preceded the noise. It was a stillness and quiet in the mind as if someone had turned off all the sounds of life, and then after a few seconds, the ringing started. In one case, I never heard any ringing. It was only the silence that was so profound in my mind. And yet, the ringing could be loud enough to drown out the voice of someone speaking. I will never forget standing in Venice, Italy, overlooking St. Mark's Square, when suddenly the ringing in my ear was so loud that I did not hear my girlfriend as she spoke to me. The silence had been intense. I had a warning. I knew the sound was coming. But I didn't expect the volume level. This particular sign figured prominently at the beginning of my grief journey. However, similar to the gifts of scent, the number of occurrences slowed over time as I came to terms with my grief. Perhaps I do not need as much consoling as I did immediately following my loss. However, I suspect it may be because the spirits have found other ways to reach me.

From the beginning, David has come to me constantly while I sleep. In the first few months, he was usually just standing off to one side in my dreams, watching me as I packed moving boxes or went about my outside chores. Always just watching. As time progressed, he started to come and hold me while reassuring me that I would be fine. But none of these were the usual chaotic dreams with no discernible flow that we all have when our subconscious tries to make sense of our worlds while we sleep. No, these were visitations where the action went from A to B in a straight line, conversations flowed, and I remembered all of it very clearly when I awoke. I was an active participant as opposed to an observer. I could always recall the feel of the denim material of his shirt or the solidness of his torso beneath the shirt. He was there. I was constantly amazed and always grateful for how present he really was in my daily life.

Walking in nature was my most consistent routine to help me heal. Every day, I walked twice a day for a total of several hours. Admittedly, having a dog made this activity non-negotiable. So, I walked in rain, snow, and sunshine. I walked on ice, pavement, beach sand, and dirt paths through the woods. And it was never lost on me how good I felt after the walk, no matter the weather or the route. Nature has always been my happy place. It is where I clear my head and contemplate life; the place where I connect with other living, breathing things, ground myself to the earth, and fully exhale. It is where I feel rejuvenated as I absorbed the energy from the ocean, lake, or river beside me.

I recall the first person who picked up on the healing effects of walking in nature upon me. The woman was reading me psychically.

"You are a beach person," she said. "I see you walking on the boardwalk, very early, in the cool air. You receive healing from it and a sense of peace."

As she spoke, I remembered how in the months immediately following his death, before I moved from the beach, I had walked the boardwalk very early every morning, just trying to hold the pieces of myself together. I was trying to heal myself. It was the only sense of peace I felt all day. But I didn't know at the time that I was not walking alone. In fact, there was a crowd walking with me. They were trying to heal me too.

The first medium to mention that I did not walk alone had brought David through, and she was not far into the reading when she stopped.

"He walks with you in nature where you walk where it is wild, not just wild from weeds, but there are bull rushes," she said. "David says to look for the bull rushes." That was not hard. As it turned out, bull rushes were everywhere along the riverbank on my preferred route at the time.

The next medium was even more specific.

"You walk at a hillside where it is green," she said. "There is a cliff. It is your walking route, and you walk it alone. It is your thinking time. He is with you when you do this. He is with you in your thoughts."

It did not take much effort to bring this picture to mind. I live on the edge of a river valley. Every morning, I descend to the base of the cliff to walk among the trees beside the water. It is not some area I just happened upon. Rather, I bought my house specifically to be able to access this area.

Between the bull rushes lining my path and the butterflies flitting about, I knew David and my mother were walking with me. I suspected there were others as well, and I was right. Apparently, my brother James is there too. One morning, after a nasty storm the night before, I ventured down my usual path. A tree had been felled by lightning and blocked the route. However, it simply took a little effort to go under the trunk and continue along. On the way back, it was another story. I fell and hit my glasses on the pavement, which saved me from hitting my head. But I had a small gash above my brow and a pair of broken eyeglasses. Several months later, a medium gave me a reading, and she connected with my brother. It was the first time he had come through a medium to me.

"He talks about your glasses being new or being repaired, glasses being fixed," she said. "He likes your new glasses. He was there with you when you fell, and they broke." For the record, I did get the broken glasses fixed, and at the same time, I purchased a new pair.

As the open circle classes progressed, my development improved. During one meditation, I saw myself sitting on a bench. A man stood beside me. He was laughing and smiling at me. I felt that he was clearly pleased with me. I did not recognize him. I asked who he was, and he said, "David."

"You're fine," he said next. "Just go forward."

The sensation of sadness cascading over me made me cry. In the end, I saw myself sitting on the bench with my head down. Six to eight people stood in a semi-circle, looking down at me. Their clothing was not discernible, but I knew there were men and women present. They were not connecting with me but rather with each other. When I emerged from the meditation later, the medium in charge of the session spoke to me. She described the scene that I had seen as I had seen it. She said she could see they were holding me up. And that was when I knew for sure that a team on the other side was working with me, trying to help me in any way they could.

In addition to the family members who walk with me, other entities from the other side walk with me too. We all have a number of guides, and we share them with others. There is always a main guide from before birth that helps us through our life to achieve whatever we set out to accomplish when we came to earth. This guide also acts as a gatekeeper and watches over additional guides who work with us throughout our life. Each guide brings its strengths and expertise, from providing extra support to gifting us specialized knowledge. Sometimes we know who our guides are, and sometimes we do not. The name of a guide is not important except to our ego.

Guides have higher intelligence than family members. So, our family members may be present to give love, support, and encouragement, but they are not guides. In my case, several family members have indicated that they are helping me with specific parts of my spiritual development work, but in no way are they guides. Personally, my knowledge of my own guides is scant. Although a medium did bring through a guide for me recently.

"He's a very tall, strong man who knows his own power," she said. "He has been with you for a little while. He's coming through to let you know he is around because you don't know he is around. He is here for strength. You have had to learn to be stronger emotionally. You have gone through life quite a strong person and then had a knockback with your husband passing away. Now you know what strength is and why you need it, and that's why he's bringing it for you. He is holding you up when you feel wobbly. When you feel wobbly, if you think of him, he will hold you up and give you that strength to carry on."

So, although I may appear as a woman and her dog to the people who pass me on my walks, I know that I do not walk alone. Many spirits walk with me as I try to heal. It is just that nobody can see them. But I know they are there and that in itself is a comfort. That is yet another form of spiritual healing.

When I first met David, his father was the groundskeeper for the city's psychiatric hospital. The hospital provided him with a house on the grounds. I always felt it was a magical place to live as it was like living in the country, in the middle of a city. But that meant it was also a good half-mile walk from the street the buses ran on, most of it up a road bordered by very tall two-hundred-year-old trees. One night, early in our dating relationship, we went to see his parents. And we walked up that road.

And it was foggy. It was not the romantic wisps one finds misting at the seashore but rather an all-encompassing dense grayness resting on the snow. It was physical in its presence. Part of the way up the road, I realized that I could no longer see where I had come from nor where I was going; not even the towering trees I knew were beside me. I saw none of it. Just fog. It was like walking in an alternative universe populated by only the two of us. But I was okay. I had no unease. I felt safe, already enveloped in the promise of young love.

I have often considered that walk a turning point in my life. If I could have seen behind me, it would have been clear that I was leaving my childhood behind. No problem, it was time. If I could have seen ahead, I would have seen the path I was choosing. But I could not see it. So, I was forging ahead fearlessly, in blind faith that I would make it to my destination. And I was doing it hand in hand with my love. I knew that it wouldn't ever matter if I had a clear view of the future or not. It would all be okay as long as he was with me.

One night recently, I walked my dog in the fog. And it took me back to that night. This fog was not quite as dense, and there were breaks. I could partially see where I had come from as the mist floated around me. And it occurred to me that even though I could not see the past as clearly as I might have liked, perhaps there was no added value to be found in trying to see history any clearer. Maybe the memory-laden fragments that made up my past were just best released as they were. I did not need to fully understand every part of my grief journey to let parts of it go. It was time.

More importantly, I could see the path ahead, also shrouded in swatches of moving grayness. Not totally clear, but at least an outline. And I thought of how once before, I walked on, not knowing where the path led, and it turned out more than fine. Why couldn't that happen again? He was still holding my hand.

And it occurred to me that walking out of grief was like walking out of a fog. I could not see all or most of the road. But it didn't matter. I steeled myself, grabbed a little courage, and put one foot in front of the other. Eventually, the fog cleared, the sun shone, and I was walking forward. I moved beyond the chaos of my previous life and discovered a new life. Going forward, all I needed to do was trust my intuition, listen to my soul, and accept the support of those who walked with me. And as I emerged from the darkness and turned a corner, I arrived at the start of a new path.

8. A NEW PATH

If only grief were linear. How many times did I wish for this? Often I thought if it just went from horrific to doable in a straight line, maybe, just maybe, I could do this. But it doesn't. Not only does it not go in a straight line, but I experienced significant portions of it repeatedly, reliving it slightly differently each time. It was a hard lesson to learn.

I truly believed that the process would be a one-and-done exercise if I sat with my grief, let it settle, and absorbed it into myself for many months. I thought there would be further contemplation at different times, but nothing like the soul-searching experience of the early days. I thought once I got through a significant amount of grief work, I would have a start on a bit of a map for the future and my place in it. But that isn't how grief works. This process seemed destined to repeat itself with regularity, like a variation on a theme.

Professionals who deal with grieving children talk about re-grief, where the children grieve differently at successive points in their childhood. This results from changes in their communication skills, cognitive abilities, coping mechanisms, and triggering life events as they age. Being a mature, developed adult, I figured this would never happen to me. But it did. And maybe that is because those factors that apply to children also apply to adult grievers at different stages of their grief journey. My ability to talk, think, and cope was barely functioning when I undertook the first deep dive into where

I belonged in this new world post-loss. Perhaps that is why, after the fog cleared, I re-examined this question anew.

The fact is it was exhausting. I was bone-weary from wondering how and where I fit. It was like trying to catch smoke. I was just plain tired of being a displaced person whose displacement recurred whenever I thought I had secured purchase. I missed the carefree days of my previous life where this was never a consideration.

What next? I thought constantly.

It would have been far less stressful if the whole road map of my life had been laid before me where I could have seen it. I had never been one for trips to the unknown, certainly not trips where, at the very least, I didn't know the destination. Equally, I always liked to see the route. I got quite unsettled when I embarked on a journey where I could not see the road in front of me. This time, there were too many roads. I didn't know which one to take. I wanted someone to tell me. I was tired of figuring it all out by myself. I searched for the clarity that escaped me on this question. It seemed the usual method of getting information to help me make decisions had failed me. There was too much information this time, and it overwhelmed me.

Three months after David died, I attended a mediumship demonstration. Two friends came with me for emotional support. We sat in a nondescript hotel conference room with about eighty other hopefuls as the two mediums took turns working. I had only seen demonstrations where the medium identified whom they would speak with directly. However, that night, the working style was to provide evidence from the spirit connection and have people raise their hands if the information resonated with them. Then those same people lowered their hands as subsequent information did not. This style was more like a process of elimination, no better or worse than any other style, just different. One medium mentioned in passing that the spirits were lined up on the other side, vying eagerly for their chance to come through. People, who were desperate for a connection, tried to make the evidence fit their loved ones. Still, when it ultimately became clear that it did not, there were dashed hopes on the part of many audience members. The scene was chaotic, and that description might even be charitable. I had no faith David would show up. I could not see him entering into this fray.

There was a short intermission, and then one of the mediums said she would do a quick round. That meant that instead of doing the more in-depth readings that average about ten minutes, these would be fast connections of a minute or less. At one point in the first hour, she had admitted that she rarely got names. So when she started the session, I was taken aback by her words.

"A man is stepping forward, and he says his name is David," she said.

I could hear the sharp intake of breath by each of my friends. Several hands went up, including my own.

"He is showing me he had chest pains when he died. And there was a motorcycle involved."

All the other hands went down. I could feel my friends put a hand on me from either side as the medium looked at me.

"He says you're doing well. You are doing better than you think you are," she said. "Keep going, like a step at a time. There is a little bit more positivity in life, in general, with each day going forward."

It was comforting to hear him say he thought I was doing well. I felt like I was hanging onto my sanity by a thread, and honestly, I had no idea how I was doing. I only knew what I was doing. The prior three months had been hectic. I had finished a house renovation, sold the house, and bought a home in another city. I gave the contents of his garage to an auctioneer because I had no idea what I now owned or what it was worth. I disposed of two trucks, one trailer, a Harley, and an RV in another country. Then I purchased a new car. I spent my days packing up the contents of the house when I wasn't tending the extensive grounds to keep them looking good. As I did it all in the throes of grief, it had never occurred to me I was doing any of it well. But there he was, making it clear to me. I was taking steps and moving forward. Such is the healing power of messages from the other side as given by mediums.

This same medium later sent out an email offering a reading comprising the answer to one question to be asked of a particular deceased loved one. The answer would come over Christmas. Merry Christmas to me, I thought. I sent off my question, which was, of course, for David. I couldn't even plan my days at the time, but I knew I needed a plan for the rest of my life. So my question was easy.

"What do you think would be the best use of my time going forward to optimize my journey?"

The answer came back several days later.

"Hello Diane, when I connect with the requested loved one, David, he comes in as what feels like a younger man. An adult, certainly, but not elderly. People would say he was young to pass, gone too soon idea. Hopefully, you understand that."

Check.

"When I ask the best use of your time from now on to optimize your journey, he says that you are having a hard time finding things to do that interest you and feel meaningful. He makes me feel like everything is just sort of plateaued with no big 'ups.' It's hard to get excited or eager, and he says sometimes it just feels like you're passing the days with no real meaning. Hopefully, you can understand that."

Check.

"One thing for sure he is saying is to keep connected to people. He says you can tend to go quiet and not reach out to folks. Meanwhile, time moves the quickest and most meaningfully when you personally are sharing it with other people. He is referencing work, he says. Funny enough, despite what we are doing here in this reading, he is saying to me that you have wisdom you have garnered through this loss. While you are still working on it, there is wisdom enough to share. And in fact, he shows me you are speaking with or counseling someone on their own loss. Begin speaking, he says. You will be surprised by what comes out. David references something like a grief group, and he makes me feel that attending something like this would benefit you. However, there are also those out there who would benefit from you being there. Share your wisdom, he says."

Check.

"Write about your journey, he says, to get it organized in your head and to allow for expression that isn't always filtered. Just get it out. He says you will become inspired by connecting with and expressing your wisdom and experiences thus far with others. This opens doors and pathways that you may not be able to see at this time. And you won't until you begin to share yourself with others (strangers, he's saying) in a way that's different than what you've done before."

Huh?

When I returned to my weekly grief support group meeting after the holidays, one of the facilitators suggested I should start writing to help process my grief. Journaling is often recommended for grievers to focus their thoughts, express their feelings, and potentially feel better. I was not convinced. I had never been a person who wrote for myself. I never even had a diary as a child. The fact is, I used to write for a living, but legal writing is a totally different type of writing from what was being described to me. Finally, I decided to give it a try. It was only a few weeks before I graduated from notepads to bound journals. I had journals for different types of writing, such as dreams, memories, and essays. But it was the essays that were the most profound for me. I would get an idea that would continue to come back to me for days before I would sit down for fifteen minutes, and the story would pour out of me. After editing, I would post them to an online grief group site I followed, and people would comment on how I had just put their feelings into words. They found the stories healing. It never occurred to me I was following David's advice. I was, unbeknownst to me, starting down the path of my new life. But there was more to come.

The following February, I was sound asleep one night until suddenly, I wasn't. A large orange funnel-shaped light lit up in my head. It felt like it had been blasted into my mind. The sound of it crashing into my brain was what actually woke me up. It sounded like a gunshot, but inside my head. I lay in the darkness and the silence, wondering what it meant. I had no doubt that it was sent from the other side but from who exactly was a mystery. More importantly, the meaning of it totally escaped me. I wasn't afraid, but I was perplexed. The following August, I was in an airplane taxiing down a runway when I saw an orange funnel-shaped windsock. It was fully extended, with the setting sun beaming through the middle. I immediately recalled the dream, but I thought that if this was a sign, I still had no idea what it meant. It would be two years before I would find out.

Meanwhile, I continued writing my essays. Then I met with a medium who brought it back to the front and center. She had been interpreting a tarot card spread when David came to her. She promptly ignored the cards.

"He is showing me a pen and paper, and he says to write a book. Write to him. He will read it," she said.

"Don't hold back is what I am hearing," she continued. "Listen to the advice you give to others. You would tell them to write the book. It would be cathartic, and then whatever you do with it would be up to you. It would help you, and if it only helps one person, great! Obviously, it is something people need. This will be well received, but it will be intense and personal when released to the world."

I was beginning to get the message, but it was not the whole message. And it wasn't until the following year, when the lockdowns were put in place due to Covid, that I understood. It wasn't until then that I ramped up my search for my path. I didn't even realize I was doing it. Suddenly, all sorts of things were more readily available online than ever before: online courses, classes, workshops, meetings, and so on. Some offerings were synchronistic. And some were just advertising thrown at me because I provided my email address to someone. It didn't matter. I was coming across the choices effortlessly. Many of them were free or so cheap that they may as well have been free. I signed up for open circle meetings. I watched mediumship demonstrations. I explored classes in so many different spiritual practices that a friend affectionately called me a "spiritual junkie." I attended Sunday services with a local Spiritualist church from the comfort of my living room. None of it felt like work. It was fascinating, exhilarating, and calming. What I did not realize at the time was that when we feel passion for our pursuits, that is when we know we are on our path. I was finally on my path.

Buoyed by my enjoyment of these classes, I briefly dipped my toes into an online writing group. It wasn't nearly as interesting as my other classes. I realized that I had gotten what I needed to get out of writing just by crafting my stories. So, my writing took a back seat to my submersion in all things spiritual for months.

One day, David came through to a classmate in a class.

"He is following up to make sure you do something with a deadline," she said. I thanked her for the message. In my arrogance and naivete, I tried to ignore his message.

The following week I got to work with her again. Before we even started the assignment we were supposed to be working on, she indicated that David was there and he was laughing. He wanted to know if I was "following through on my writing."

I capitulated. I took a course on writing a book, another offering that mysteriously appeared in my inbox. I collected all of my essays together and tried to see what kind of book I could make out of them. As much as the essays were a love story, they also set out the trajectory of my grief journey. I scoured my textbooks and notes from the thanatology courses I had taken at university the past few semesters and put together a book. *Demystifying Grief: What You Need to Know to Heal* was to be my offering to the world, spilling out the secrets of grief. But I was having trouble with one chapter, so I booked a session with the medium who ran the spiritual development class I attended for some guidance.

"David is talking about a chapter in your book," she started. "He's really chuffed that you are dedicating the book to him because it comes from the heart. He likes it. You just need to get it finished. He says you did not like the corners when on his motorcycle. He liked to show off with it. But it is like Spiritualism; you have to go with the flow. You have to go be in the energy and connect to the energy of it. Don't mind the corners, don't mind the curves, because you'll get there. And, by the way, there is a typo in chapter twelve."

There was, indeed, a typo in chapter twelve. But I went on to discuss the chapter of concern in detail with him through her. He even dictated part of it to me. I don't think it is a stretch to say I could not have done it without him. Before we ended our session, she asked if I had any questions.

"Well, actually," I said, "one night about two years ago, this crashing orange light exploded into my head, and the sound of it woke me up." She didn't require any more details. She took a minute, clearly concentrating on whatever David was telling her. Her answer was as illuminating as the original flash of light in the dream.

"That was David and your mother giving you something to get you onto your spiritual path and the creativity to do it. Orange is a very creative color. They were giving you something to get yourself out of your own way, and because it is you, you needed bigger proof, a bigger confirmation. You needed a slap in the face, a punch to wake you up to get you to where you needed to be because you've got another book to write, but it's different. That flash of orange was you coming to your spiritual path. It was a power surge for you. It was to get you onto your spiritual path in a bigger way and into the groups because they also sustained you through Covid. It was to get your brain working differently, thinking about things in a different way (not so black and white, so linear). Also, it was about being more aware, so you would start to notice and make connections, like showing you the windsock. It was supposed to be a more refined effect, but it was more like a three-ring circus with your mum, dad, and David all coming together."

So there it was. I finally had confirmation that I was on the correct path, and it seemed to have two distinct but intertwined portions. I was supposed to be writing to help people. My first book was just that, the first book. There was to be a second one on spiritual matters. I needed to develop my inherited second sight gifts to understand this other world first. This was in keeping with what I had been told in my only astrological chart reading.

"Your authentic self has a need to express, but it is blocked. This could be blocked because of religion, grief, or moral code," the astrologist had said. "Your soul path theme is to connect with people, not one-on-one but en masse. Now is the time to change, transform, and expand resulting from a profound change in yourself. It is almost like something had to die for this new energy to come."

Indeed, I thought, sadly. Something had died. David had died. My old life had died. I had wanted to die. Plenty of ashes were strewn over the remnants of my life for the phoenix in me to rise from.

But I had some skills to draw on. As much as I had learned to survive within my family by being silent, I also knew how to thrive outside the family, where life demanded I be more outgoing. I had lived in eight different cities in two countries by the time I went to high school. I was always the new kid in class at school. I made new friends constantly. I learned to be the one who always took the first step forward. I could step forward into the unknown. I had done it plenty of times in the past. It might not be comfortable, but I knew I could do it. I had to start somewhere.

One of the results of taking many classes in spiritual matters is that messages from the other side are given and received constantly. Those sorts of courses are run by experienced mediums. Their developed gifts are, in many cases, quite astonishing, even to the critical eye of a life-long observer such as myself. And the classes are full of people who are also exploring the limits of their own abilities. So, as I moved toward finishing the book, there was no end of messages of encouragement and support from the other side to help me get to the finish line.

In time, I finished the first book and sent it out into the world, hopefully, to help someone who may also be suffering in their own grief. Truth be told, I was not excited as such. Nothing seemed to excite me much. My level of enthusiasm seemed to be constantly capped somewhere far short of my before-his-death levels. I just wanted to finish the project and be done. Probably because I have never been a quitter. I always tied things up neatly before putting them away. Writing the book was therapeutic for me. However, I had already moved on in my head from this part of my journey. It was just as well because as soon as it was published, I got a lead on how my path would unfold next. In truth, it was less of a hint and more of a road map. After a class, I got a note from a fellow attendee who had received a message for me during the class meditation. He outlined his evidence which only confirmed his assertion that David had come through to him.

"The sense of the message was about your books," he said. "The feeling I had was, okay, you've got your first book (done and dusted!), and it's about grief (to do with the human condition). You will also write one about the spirit world experience (on the other side of the veil). But there is an opportunity for you to write another book, and it is about the transition between the two worlds and your experience of it (perhaps as a developing medium or spiritual person)."

So, there it was laid out for me; write three books. I have to admit that I had a momentary fit of pique. I felt a bit pressured to do this by a man who never wrote anything more comprehensive than a list of car parts he needed to buy when he was on this earth plane. I even said something out loud like, "If you want to write books so much, maybe you should have stayed here and done it." But that was the grief talking, and I dismissed it as soon as I heard myself say it. I knew the other side was in charge of the agenda, which suited me. It fit. And I was as passionate about the projects as they were. I had already done one, and another was off in the distance. And I had, unbeknownst to myself, already been training to write the third one by immersing myself in everything spiritual for the past two years. I knew this was my path now. I could feel it. The only thing left was to embrace it. So, I did.

My initial meditations in open circle sessions had improved over time. I progressed from seeing colors or visual scenes to hearing the occasional words from someone to feeling, say, David handing me a flower. What became apparent to me over time was that further spiritual development might just allow me to converse with David more fully without the need for a medium. Months of practice finally revealed what I could do.

The meditation was relatively simple. It just required sending energy out from the chest and then stepping outside to a favorite place in nature. Once there, we were to sit down and ask someone to come and join us. The focus of the exercise was to ask questions of the spirit(s) who came and see what answers, if any, we received. I asked what was wrong with my leg and what I should do about it because it had been quite painful for a long while. As I had so many times before, I could clearly hear the words in my head.

"Arthritis, see Dr. Don." I knew immediately that David was with me as this was how he had always referred to our family doctor, whose first name was Don. It was his personal term of endearment for him. I could feel David holding my right hand. With the practical question out of the way, I went for the bigger picture—what is it like wherever he is.

"Is it lovely there?" I asked.

"Not as lovely as you," he replied. Nice dodge, I thought. But I forgave him as I could feel the love washing over me.

"Can we go for a ride when I get there?" I asked.

"We can go for a ride," he said softly.

And I heard him as clearly as if he was alive and standing next to me on the earth plane.

That day, I learned that I could dialogue with spirits in the spirit world. I did not have to be just a passive receiver of whatever information they chose to give me. I could ask questions. Like my mother, I could talk to dead people. And I knew I could get better at it. I immediately recalled the message I had received from a medium at the previous week's Spiritualist church service.

"Your mother and father are here," she said. "And your dad is looking at me like I have three heads. He says, why do you need her? You can do this. There is no need for a third party. A brand-new door has opened, one that is very spiritually based. It has opened to the other world." In retrospect, his message had a prophetic air to it.

At the next open circle session, David was back. A woman said she got the name "David" and he was with a dog wearing a blue collar.

"He said take the next course," she said.

No one else in the circle could take this message. I thought about the fact that I had been seriously considering taking a particular spiritual development course. But I had not registered for it as I hadn't felt confident that I was ready. I looked down at David's dog, wearing her blue collar, as she lay at my feet. I immediately signed up for the course.

9. SURRENDERING

I was never big on noting the days of the week. Dates, yes, days, no. And dates fluctuate over different days, making the actual day of some events seem even less relevant. I am sure I only remember that I had my son on a Saturday because my doctor was missing in action at the big moment. I have lost a lot of people in my life; parents, siblings, in-laws, and too many friends. I could not say what day of the week any of them died. Truth be told, I have even lost some of the dates from my memory, too.

Except for David. He died on a Sunday. I am certain I will never forget this fact. And for months afterward, the day was important because it marked another week he was gone. In essence, Sunday became the measuring stick. And I hated Sundays. As awful as the rest of the week was, it was fever pitch by Saturday in anticipation of Sunday. By Sunday night, I could finally breathe again before starting the process all over again. This went on for months and months and months.

At some point, I thought I had to do something to break the cycle. So, to distract myself, I started cooking on Sundays. I made meals and baked treats for the coming week. I filled my freezer with portions of food I could grab as the week went on, never having to cook for another seven days. But at least I got through Sunday. This, too, went on for months and months. And then Sundays did not seem so awful. At least they were productive.

Then I signed up for a spiritual development course, which happened to be on a Sunday. Of all the classes I took all week, and there were many, it was my favorite. I looked forward to Sundays because I enjoyed them so much. Well into this routine, a friend asked me if I was having a good day.

"Yes," I replied. "It is Sunday. It is my fun day!"

Healing, as I have said before, comes in many forms. It wasn't until I heard my own words that I realized I had broken the hold that day of the week had had over me. I had changed my attitude about a day of the week. It was one less negative thing to carry into my new life. The feeling of freedom meshed with my change of attitude about my life.

I also realized I was approaching every situation with a heightened degree of sensitivity. I did not even want to cut wildflowers for fear of injuring the plants. I recall the feeling that came over me one day when I ventured onto my usual path in the forest. The city workers had come through the area the day before to prepare sections of a walkway for resurfacing. It looked like a logging camp. Destroyed trees lay beside the path everywhere. Stumps jutted up from the ground with jagged splinters of wood calling to the sky. Tree trunks and branches were strewn among the underbrush. A fine layer of sawdust was everywhere as if it was trying to somehow soften the effect of the carnage. I looked at the scene and felt like I had received a physical blow. The ancient Celts were animists and honored the forces of nature; the Celt in me was stunned. It pained me to walk past the remnants of such violence for weeks afterward.

Why would someone destroy nature so people could walk in even less nature? I thought. The incident reinforced how much I had changed since David had died. It showed me how my attempts to open myself up to the other side of the veil simultaneously opened up the whole of me to align with my soul. I needed to learn how to manage the side effects of this process.

When I finally acknowledged my newly expanded compassion-ate side, I understood that getting to that point had been a tough road. Most people like to think they are reasonably compassionate, and I believe I fell into that category in my pre-loss life. But there is something about experiences that bring us to our knees that up our empathy quotient. No one likes to think their loss made them more empathetic to others. But the truth is, for me, it did. It took a while to reconcile my discovery with my previously held beliefs about myself. But I noticed changes in my behavior. If I encountered someone surly or negative, I smiled and ignored their behavior. I found myself thinking that I had no idea what their lives entailed; they could be grieving for all I knew. I admonished myself if I slipped up and simply thought something judgmental. Being less critical meant I could be more open to and accepting of others.

I met many like-minded people when I started taking the many courses and workshops on all manner of spiritual pursuits. Everyone I encountered was eager, open-minded, and evolving. The first two characteristics made them good students to accompany on this journey of exploration. The last one made them good people to meet. They were not only refreshing and comfortable but inspiring, too. Despite all of the negativity traversing the world and the effects of the pandemic running rampant, the people I met were a tonic of serenity, gentleness, and gratitude. Like me, they had an increased consciousness regarding negativity. They, too, believed that one's thoughts led to actions, positive or negative, and so desired to have only positive thoughts going forward. They embraced gratitude as a guiding principle in their lives like I did. Most importantly, I learned that increased positive thoughts eventually led to leaving others behind. My new vibe demanded a new tribe.

From the first class with the Light Within spiritual development group, I knew I had found my tribe. Plain and simple, these were my people. It was a group run out of Scotland, and most group members had a Scottish brogue similar to the one my family had. They sounded familiar. They sounded like home. But more importantly, they felt like home. They felt like family at a soul level.

In addition, they embodied the quintessential characteristics of these sorts of groups. They provided a safe and supportive environment where everyone was encouraged to push their limits and work on the quality, accuracy, and content of their readings. Their patience and compassion were almost tangible. All students were there to advance their abilities. Some wanted to learn how to do readings for the general public. Others, like me, were just looking to hone their psychic and spiritual skills as an integral part of their personal growth. In the end, we would all do the same work, healing.

Several weeks after my first spiritual development class, I attended a Spiritualist church service, and the medium spoke to me.

"I feel a powerful energy around you," she said. "It is quite regularly around you. You think of Spirit, and they are all there. You hear voices as well. That is them trying to get through to you. You are stepping onto your spiritual path now. I see your mother with a cup of tea leaves, and she is handing it over to you like a baton. This goes back generations; quite a few women there would have practiced Spiritualism or talking to Spirit, or healing. It is not just your mother and grandmother; it goes back further."

It was always nice to get confirmation from the other side that I was where I was supposed to be. I was particularly touched by my mother passing the baton to me. It made me feel connected, not only to my mother and my heritage but to my new purpose in life. However, I was always cautious when I received readings like this one, where I could not confirm the evidence, in this case, descending from a long line of women with abilities. In those cases, despite the information being presented as a fact, I generally just noted the evidence and suspended my belief in the truth of it. I gave it weight if it was something I could investigate and prove on this side of the veil. If I could not confirm it, I just waited to see if another medium mentioned the same information at a different time. Belief has to make sense; one should never follow blindly. In this case, this medium was the third one to bring up a line of female ancestors and their healing powers on my mother's side. I was ready to accept the baton. It was another of the many turning points in my life. I could feel it.

The spiritual development classes differed from the open circle sessions in several ways. To begin with, they were not a drop-in format. There were no new people every week bringing in different energies. Members were required to commit to a multi-week series of classes. It was expected that we would keep our appointment with the spirit world. The class began with a lecture, and there was time for questions to be answered and concepts discussed. Then there was a guided meditation. Afterward, the participants broke off into pairs to practice the assigned exercises. There was a final gathering together at the end to discuss how it went for everyone.

To me, the number one concept that must be internalized to become a medium is that we are spiritual beings having a human experience, *not* human beings having a spiritual experience. We must accept that we are more fully integrated into life on the other side than we are into life on earth. We just don't remember much of our spiritual life while we are here on earth having our human experience. The point is that nothing is more natural than communicating with those on the other side. But it doesn't just happen for most people. It is a skill that has to be developed like any other, and as with other skills, it only gets better with practice. The aim is to become a disciplined medium who can turn their abilities on and off. A medium needs to know how to shift their awareness to the spirit world. They must recognize when they have raised the vibrational frequency of their soul high enough to receive the vibration of a spirit communicator's soul. The medium must feel the blending of their soul with that of another.

Mediumship is a uniquely individual skill despite several formulaic approaches. But the end game is the same: to increase spirit connections and the strength of those connections. One of the best ways to learn what is involved is to watch other mediums work. But the better way is to do the work oneself. When one undertakes this training, it is invariably done with enthusiasm. If we are drawn to this work, it is our time to pursue it. If Spirit wants us, Spirit will get us, bringing people into our lives to guide us. And Spirit never makes mistakes. When we are finally ready to pursue this path, our team of helpers has already been waiting in the wings for us.

It starts with meditation. We set an intention before meditating. Purposes when doing mediumship can include connecting fully with spirits, working in love and laughter, connecting with guides, and so on. It can be as specific as asking a question to get an answer or, in my case, a general request for their spiritual guidance as they deem fit. We cannot tell spirits what to do, nor can we control them. We are not the higher power in this pairing. So, I surrender to their direction. This is easier said than done for a control-freak personality like mine. But with effort, I have managed it.

We breathe in slowly, hold it for a few seconds, and exhale slowly. We try to still our minds as we repeat the process. This lets the spirits know we are ready to work. We focus on our breathing, eliminating random thoughts in the mind. We pull away from the exterior world and pull into the inner one. We shift our attention to the internal world. We mentally expand the energy using our minds. We invite spirits to blend with us. There is a difference in feeling between our own energy alone and the combined energy when a spirit has connected with us. Often the calling card can be physical sensations felt around the face and head. Just as when we work psychically and then move into mediumship, we feel the energy shift.

It all starts with us. We have increased our level of self-awareness about our own energy and become familiar with it. We must recognize when our cup is half full or depleted and not work until we feel better. We must be able to discern confidently that the information received is from a spirit and not from ourselves. Spirits communicate very fast. We think slower. So, we need to be working on all cylinders from the get-go. Otherwise, the results will be disappointing.

There are other considerations if we are working with a sitter receiving a reading from us. We have to set the intent that we will attract a spirit communicator. We mentally expand our energy and invite spirits to come in. It can be helpful if the sitter can focus on who they want to hear from. This can strengthen our link to the spirit communicator for us. When we feel the spirit communicator come forward, we say what we see, hear, feel, and so on. At this point, we are not thinking. For to be thinking means we are not linking with the spirit. We would have left the link and gone into our conscious mind. In fact, if we remember the reading, it was likely because we were working psychically. If we don't remember the reading, it resulted from mediumship. And an ethical medium will make it clear which it is. A sitter should never be unclear as to precisely who said what, the medium or the spirit communicator.

Suppose we get interrupted and lose the link. In that case, we repeat what we have already said to rebuild the energy and reinforce the connection. We have to keep moving and talking to keep the energy high. Sometimes, we must take a minute and breathe into the spirit to bring them closer. So, the breathe, surrender, and blend exercise may have to be repeated during a reading if the energy gets too low, or the link weakens.

There are many different reasons that a link can weaken. Asking questions of the spirit communicator can weaken the link. Psychic and remote viewing work done amid a reading can break the connection. To do those techniques, we retreat psychically within our own energy, not dealing with the spirit communicator at that point. Checking in with the sitter too much can also weaken our connection. In that case, our energy can blend with the sitter instead of keeping with the spirit communicator. That is why we prefer it if the sitter only gives a yes or no response to the information provided. If it is something the sitter cannot take, we try to say it differently, but negative responses will cause us to move along. The sitter or we may misinterpret the information, or it may be unknown to the sitter. Doing a deep dive into it will cause us to start thinking and lose the link. Long pauses can weaken the link, so we try to keep the energy moving by talking. Sometimes, we may ask the sitter if they have any questions. This is usually done at the end when the connection is the strongest. Equally, the message for the sitter is often given at the end. And since spirits do not just come to say hello, but rather for a specific reason, we want to keep the link as strong as possible to ensure the entire message is conveyed. Although one thing I have learned is that if the information is essential, the spirit communicator will bring it back to me, sometimes differently, until I share it.

Readings usually take the same form. We first identify the spirit communicator who is coming through to speak. Next, we will provide evidence from the spirit regarding their traits when on the earth plane, such as physical description, occupation, personality, and so on. The spirit communicator may share some fond memories or acknowledge some event that occurred after their passing. Finally, we focus on the message they want to give. To get all this, we use every sense we can: seeing, hearing, tasting, feeling, knowing, and so on. Some work better than others for different people, and they can change over time. None are any more important than another; we just focus on the strongest ones we have and develop them first. Of course, we do not use them all at once because that would be overwhelming. We would be unable to focus and receive the information. But we use them individually in different parts of the reading. And just as the strengths of the various clairs differ for all of us, how they are used also varies by the reader.

For me, clairvoyance is one of my stronger abilities. This is where I see images in my mind or something from the corner of my eye. Many mediums work with symbology which means, for example, when they see a white rose, it means that someone is offering love to the sitter. I haven't progressed in that manner. I simply see images in my head as if a movie is playing. Often in conjunction with the images, I experience claircognizance where I just know information about the images. Still, I do not know how I know it. This information can be from the past, present, or future. My clairsentience picks up on the emotions of the people I am seeing. This is where I feel something to be true. I just get a sense of something. I also experience strong clairaudience, where I hear sounds inside my head. It may be someone speaking, or it may be music.

I remember one particularly poignant reading I gave where I used all of my clairs. It was a complete sensory experience. As always, I started with a feeling that gave me a gender. Spirit communicators present as they were on earth, so the energy is gender identifiable. Male and female energies feel different to me. I knew the energy was male, but as he drew close, I could see him. He was a handsome young man, standing tall, dressed casually, and looking serious. I described him in detail to the sitter. Then I explained their relationship to one another. That I just knew. Next, I felt pain as if my body had been slammed into something hard. Just as I felt the jolt, the man spoke in my mind.

"I didn't mean for it to happen. Just miscalculated," the man said.

I heard him say it so clearly. And I knew his sudden death was an unfortunate, tragic accident that took him too young.

Then the tone of the reading changed. I suddenly saw the sitter leaning back into a rattan love seat on her porch in the evening. She was surrounded by lush plants and flowers, and I was aware that she was listening to a radio on the table beside her. She was doing some sort of craft work with her hands. It was not the sort of hobby that required concentration or counting stitches, like fine needlework, but rather it was a task where she could let her mind wander as she did it. Then I saw him sitting on the love seat with his arm around her, watching her. I just knew he did this often. And just as the pain had come when he was communicating about the accident, it was a feeling of sadness this time. It was overpowering. I recognized the waves of her grief as they washed over me, as he sat there absorbing her sorrow. I started to cry. I pulled myself together just as the waves of despair immediately stopped. They were followed by an outpouring of warmth as he shared his love to comfort her. I got incredibly warm, but the sitter mentioned she could feel the heat before I got a chance to tell her. He said how much he had always loved her and loved her still. He did not want her to be so sad.

She confirmed that the evidence I had given her was correct, and she was grateful for his message. It was apparent that something in the reading gave her some measure of comfort. What precisely did not matter to anyone but her. I was content to know the reading gave her some measure of healing. In other words, I was glad the reading had done what they should always do; be uplifting and leave the sitter with the feeling of love and a sense that they are not alone. Hopefully, they also hear a few memories that make them smile.

Interestingly, just a few weeks before I gave this reading, I spoke with a friend who is a medium about spirituality, mediumship, and healing. I had pointed out to her that I had no desire to work as a medium, have clients, or do demonstrations. I had not undertaken this journey for any reason beyond purely and simply wanting to talk to my family in the spirit world. She just smiled.

"Every time you take a class, and you are working, you are giving valid messages to other people," she said. "You are helping and healing. It is where your heart is leading you. You are usually analytical but are more heart-centered now. As you move forward, you will trust more. You will be more receptive to things. You are opening up more and more. It is not just about learning, but rather about receiving and giving."

Yet, I learned something new every time I did a reading. I discovered new or improved abilities and learned about presentation, such as how to manage my emotions and not cry. One lesson I learned early on was to say exactly what I heard or saw. No paraphrasing was allowed. The way the information is communicated to a medium by the spirit communicator is precise. Changing the words can change the meaning of what was said or make the information seem irrelevant. I learned this the hard way when I changed the thought in my head to seemingly make more sense before conveying it to the sitter. The sitter did not relate to what I said at all. Afterward, during our debriefing session, I repeated the phrase exactly as I had heard it. It made perfect sense to the sitter then. I learned that the reading might have gone entirely differently if I had just trusted what was said and repeated it verbatim. There was so much to learn.

All mediums are psychics, but not all psychics are mediums. Psychics perceive information from a sitter. We work with the sitter's energy and sometimes use tools like tarot cards. Mediums, on the other hand, receive information from the spirit of someone who has passed. And to receive information, we must trust and surrender as mediums. We have to trust that spirits will show up for us, that they will provide good, relevant information, and that it will help the sitter. But to trust to this level, every medium has to shift their ego to the side. We must surrender to a higher power and believe we will be used by that power for the greater good. This most important lesson, surrendering to Spirit, was also the hardest for me. I have never left anything to chance in my life. I constantly analyzed all possible outcomes of any situation and controlled every situation as best I could. Giving up control has never been my strong suit.

In particular, I have always been apprehensive about performing mediumship when children presented as the spirit communicator in any reading I gave. I was very aware that if a child had passed, the pain for the sitter could be immense, and I never wanted to add to that burden. I feared my inexperience would cause me to provide an uncomfortable experience for the sitter. However, when I started to trust and surrender more, I realized that a spirit communicator would not come through presenting as a child if I was not able to deliver the message in an appropriately sensitive manner. So I just practiced and held them in a space of love. And I trusted Spirit to ensure the sessions would go smoothly. And they did.

I recall several readings I received around that time that were almost carbon copies of one another. Whereas at the beginning of my journey, I received unending messages focusing on my broken heart, grief, and sadness, now the messages from my family on the other side were relentless about my lack of trust.

"You have a gift. Are you a medium?" asked the medium. "Trust what they are giving you. There is a neon sign above your head saying *trust*. Don't let anyone discourage this spiritual journey you are on. David says you're going to be a gift to all those you help through your service of spirit."

And, "They are drawing really close to you," said my classmate. "They are quite keen to work with you. You have a natural ability to do healing. Trust, trust, trust. You are not finally there yet because you're not sure about it. You should be doing more. Maybe spiritual healing."

The fact is healing is universal energy available to all who ask for it. We have different guides for healing than for spiritual development. But we do not have to work with any of them in isolation from the others. We must build relationships with all of our guides and ask for their help. We need to sustain a higher vibration to connect with them because they bring gifts for us to develop. We need to trust in their wisdom and surrender to their direction.

I healed myself on my grief journey with help from those on the other side. It only seems right to pay it forward any way that I can. Perhaps, going forward, I may be able to help someone heal. Or maybe my journey will inspire someone to heal themselves. Either option is a win.

10. A CHANCE TO HELP

I had a great mother-in-law. She was like a mother hen whose brood kept coming back for more. Because she was a giver. She gave of her time, energy, creativity, and hard work to make sure everyone in her orbit felt loved. Probably because seeing the effects of her love was enough pleasure for her. She ran charity bazaars and church receptions when she wasn't making something for the family. I often walked into her kitchen to find her preparing dozens of sandwiches, deviled eggs, and butter tarts for a reception in the church hall. Serving and giving to others was the driving force in her life. In the thirty-eight years I knew her, I only remember her asking me to do something for her twice.

The first Christmas I went to her home was like landing in Santa's workshop. Cats and dogs were running about. Home-baked goodies were everywhere. She was still putting the finishing touches on a gift or two. The aromas wafting through the house told me dinner was prepped and ready to go. And she was totally unflustered as she moved from one task to another with military precision. All offers to help were declined. I suspect we would have just been in her way. At some point in the preceding year, I had indicated that I was not a fan of turkey. I was genuinely shocked when she presented me with a small Cornish hen for my dinner plate. But she was like that. She listened when people spoke, and then she thought of ways she could make them feel more comfortable and loved.

She was immensely creative. No craft endeavor was beyond her grasp. She gave everything a whirl, from crocheting to ceramic work to painting silk scarves. The year she did stained glass, she made a four-by-five-foot angel to hang in her front window with the remainder of the nativity scene sitting below it. It was a magnificent piece of art. And every Christmas, family members would receive her latest creations, including but not limited to a cloth nativity scene, knitted mittens, a ceramic chess set, a miniature village, and a hand-painted sleigh. Each year, I couldn't wait to see what she had made, and I was always thrilled that she had taken the time to create these keepsakes for us. I treasure them still.

As much as she "did crafts," as she saw it, by far and away her natural talent was sewing. She made innumerable Hallowe'en costumes for the kiddos. (I never had to make one, thanks very much.) And she made fancy dresses each Christmas for the girls. I stayed with her when I needed a wardrobe for a week of articling interviews. She made me five outfits to wear—matching plaid lines, covering buttons, and ensuring every outfit had a jacket. She just wanted to do whatever she could to help me in my new career. But her specialty was wedding dresses, and she made them for free. If the bride couldn't find a suitable pattern, my mother-in-law simply made the pattern first. Before I married, I bought everything from a pattern and material to interfacing and thread. I shipped it across the country to her. She arrived two days before the wedding with the finished dress in hand, no alterations required. I often recall the moment at her funeral as the minister spoke fondly of her.

"Raise your hand if Betty made you a wedding dress," he said.

Nearly two dozen hands went up. I can still see my husband's smile at this; her legacy was one of giving.

But the giving I remember her most fondly for was the gift of life to her son and ultimately him to me. She raised him right; he was polite, hard-working, respectful, grateful, and also a giver. He understood the importance of love and generosity. He wasn't like that by chance. It resulted from being raised in a family where love and giving were fundamentals and demonstrated as such. So, as she lay dying, I thanked her for my husband, for he was her greatest gift to me.

I believe that like attracts like, as my mother-in-law's life demonstrated. Putting good things out into the universe results in good things returning to us. I genuinely believe this. But I also understand how many people may not believe this. After all, many of us have had life experiences that we neither wanted nor deserved. In the aftermath of a death or other tragedy, it can be hard to retain, or worse, to have to create a positive attitude towards life and its offerings. And when we can barely help ourselves, it can be hard to motivate ourselves to help others. However, I think it is worth the effort. The satisfaction of offering our gifts to others also uplifts us.

I have always been a glass-half-full girl. I admit I was dealt a good hand, but I also consciously made the most of what I was handed from a young age. I never presumed that the Wheel of Fortune would not turn downward for me. And it did, many times, but it always turned back up, often when I least expected it to. I learned at a very early age to not take any of it for granted, to expect nothing, and to be grateful for all of it. But somewhere along the line, I also learned that helping others felt good.

For most of my life, I have primarily worked in what are referred to as the helping professions. Fresh out of college, I worked on city streets counseling youth in an outreach capacity for a free medical-social clinic operating at the time. As much as I may have helped someone in that job, I think perhaps I was the one who was helped the most. That job deepened my understanding that we are all not so fortunate in this life. There is no level playing field. People are just trying to survive the obstacles of life. Accordingly, judgment should be left at the door permanently. A helping hand should be extended at every opportunity. After all, we are all in this together.

When I became a lawyer, the inequities of life were even more apparent. More than once, I heard myself say, "How does the person with no resources, no legal expertise, and perhaps no proper command of the English language deal with this?" Even in minor matters of everyday life, I could see where many people had no hope of navigating a problem to their benefit. Early in my career, I met a young man in my office. He had a minor developmental issue, and he was distraught. He came in because he was a victim of identity theft in the days before it was even a recognized term. He had no idea what to do. The thief had even managed to get a driver's license in this fellow's name even though my client was not medically cleared to drive. It took quite a while to sort through the quagmire that was his life on paper. But we did it. I didn't have the heart to charge him for my work. To this day, his case remains my fondest memory of an accomplishment in my legal career. I got to help someone make their life less complicated, just a little better. There is something extremely gratifying about being an advocate for people who need special support because they cannot, for whatever reason, comprehend the things they need to.

I am always aware that my first book (on grief) was born out of the most tragic event of my life. And I have received feedback that I never sought out nor expected regarding how it has helped people in similar circumstances. I simply wrote to help myself survive the worst moments of my life and then made it into a book to hopefully help others do the same. I just put it out there to the universe with good intentions. And positive reactions have come back to me. Like I said, I believe like attracts like. This is a benefit of helping others. I am sure my mother-in-law would say that she always received far more in return for her efforts than she ever gave out.

My immersion into Spiritualism, another helping profession, is a new path for me, but it is also my old path. It was the whisperings I remember from my childhood. It was the nemesis ever-present in my teen years, threatening to expose me when I was going astray. In later years, it was something of interest for short periods when the mood struck me and I had the time to look into it. It came to be my salvation in my life's most painful moments, those moments when I found myself on my knees. It is interesting how things keep coming around until we finally pay attention and seize them.

Meanwhile, life is full of negative and positive things placed in our path. Even though we find comfort in familiarity versus the unknown, eventually we have to take a chance and fly. In my case, I had to take the plunge. I looked hard at who I was, where I came from, and where I was going next. I returned to my true self, the girl who revealed only glimpses of herself to others throughout her life. I came home to my soul. And I am sure this is why I have heard Scotland calling to me since I stepped onto this new path. Every day, I think of Scotland and say, "I need to go home." And I know in my heart it is not a case of if I go to Scotland, but rather when.

I have had many messages that tell me that spirits are guiding me on my new path. I am not surprised by this, and I am sure it was due to their intervention that I made it to the Light Within spiritual development group. This group has helped me in more ways than I can say. They have offered friendship, learning, and a safe, non-judgmental space within which to practice and learn. Most of all, they have taught me to trust the process, the results, and myself. They have shown me that there are no stupid questions, just ones not asked yet. And they have demonstrated a patience that seems unending for those of us on the first steps of this journey. It is a joy to spend a few hours a week among so many who seem devoid of ego and bring no competitiveness to the class.

This has been a journey I have needed to take for a very long time. I was always aware it was there but never chose to get on the path and try it on for size. I am so glad to have done so in the comfort of this group. The compassion shown has been unending. I have appreciated all of the help and tips received. Learning from those so invested in their journeys has proven to be a godsend.

I have not only been able to recognize and nurture my abilities, but the group has forced me to take a broader view of my life path. I am not always sure where it is headed, but I feel confident that with my newly discovered self, from now on, I will, at the very least, always be on the correct path. It is hard to fall off the path with so many on both the earth and spiritual planes cheering me on.

Currently, there is an increased interest in Spiritualism in North America. It has coincided with people turning away from the traditional Christian religions. In Spiritualism, the focus is on personal responsibility for oneself and actions here on earth. There are no rituals, penances, or special prayers to absolve us of our missteps. It is all up to us, individually, to live our lives in kindness. It is also up to us to serve Spirit. One way to accomplish these tasks is to be the voice of Spirit and speak kindness whenever possible. We have nothing to lose by trying this. Even from the like attracts like perspective, at the very least, if we send kindness out to the world, I feel sure it will come back to us. However, more importantly, I also believe that the kindness we send out into the world can lead to kindness multiplying and spreading even further. We need to live it and speak of it whenever we can. Living kindly is one thing but spreading the words so others can consider if they may wish to do this too is another. Both are important.

Another way to serve Spirit is to practice ethical mediumship. Providing evidence of life after death and healing messages is done through us, not by us. It is a spirit providing the words, the messages, and the healing. We are, so correctly named, just the medium through which spirits deliver their healing. But we are also the gatekeeper. We must feel into whether a person will be receptive or not to a message. If a spirit comes, we may have to ask them to step back until the right moment to approach the recipient occurs.

We must also ask consent to work with someone every time. The medium uses many techniques to do a reading accurately, including remote viewing, which looks into a person's life. Permission to do this is critical. We must own whether the information comes from psychic powers, mediumship, or conscious reasoning. We must guard against anyone thinking our comments from psychic or conscious reasoning result from mediumship. Finally, mediums have to be clear that they are not medical diagnosticians. Mediumship is a helping profession that only extends as far as pointing people in the right direction toward clinical experts. Spiritual healing should not be viewed as a substitute for medical treatment by a physician.

But when it comes down to it, Spiritualism and mediumship are just other ways to help people. Most people do not come to Spiritualism looking for a medium for entertainment purposes. They come looking to heal. And mediumship is a way to provide some comfort to the suffering. And just as with other helping professions providing comfort to the sorrowful, mediums will often say that their work is immensely gratifying. I cannot agree more.

Not quite five months after my husband died, I moved to a new house mainly because it had access to paths through the forest beside a river. And I walked those paths twice a day, just his dog and me. This routine saved my life. It saved me from going down the rabbit hole of grief. I am a girl who has only ever found peace in nature; the surroundings soothe me. And over the years, I noticed that I ran into the same people who also walked regularly; kindred spirits out there for the same reason as me or for various other reasons. There was no doubt about it. There was a legion of souls out there trying to clear their heads and make sense of their lives.

I knew this from the odd conversation I had here and there from which I could surmise some life angst or, in one case, an outright admission of "I am out here to clear my head." And this fellow troubled me. I saw him several times a week for months and months, and, unlike the many others I ran into, there was never a lively exchange with him, not even a smile. Then I met him as we both braved a driving snowfall to walk. My dog immediately gravitated to him, moving closer to receive a pat. She does this often. She seems to have an uncanny ability to ferret out the people we come across who need to pat her. I sensed he needed it, too. She stood stock still for him. She looked at me, and I could see in her eyes that she was telling me that this man needed some compassion. She was going nowhere despite the mounting layer of snowflakes on her jacket.

"Some puppy therapy," he said shakily as he straightened up after tousling her ears.

I smiled and waited—I could feel it, more was coming.

"My wife's funeral is tomorrow," he said very quietly.

And there it was. I was offered a chance to help on a forest path amidst a snowstorm. He was crying, and I knew I could not walk away. Of course, I offered and he accepted some tissues. (We grievers always have tissues at the ready, no matter where we are.)

I tried to do all the right things. I tried to say nothing that might offend his heightened sensitivities due to grief. I asked his wife's name, and then I just listened, which allowed him to share whatever he could communicate at that moment. He told me about her cancer, the treatments, the hope, the dashed dreams, and the anticipatory grief. There was a sense of pleading in his voice as he said he just wanted her back and that seven years of marriage was not nearly enough. He talked about a trip they had taken to Mexico. And he mentioned how he teased her that she was hedging her bets when she had kept her own last name. I could only imagine the love, the shock, and the sorrow, but it was not hard. I am too familiar with a lot of the lanes on this highway. After half an hour or more, we finally parted.

"Thanks for taking the time to listen," he said.

And once again, I was reminded how, especially in the early days of grief, any griever just wants to be heard, to have someone listen to and hear them. This man needed that, and I was grateful to have been of service in that regard. Actions demonstrate caring. Being kind, as well as offering support and assistance, are ways to help someone heal. Offering support and providing help can take many forms, from walking someone's dog to doing several loads of laundry for them. Dropping off meals is a time-honored tradition for a reason. Making time to just sit with a cup of tea and listen to someone who needs an ear can be an invaluable gift. Helping and healing does not always require a unique skill set. We simply need to turn our minds to it. Honestly, I never foresaw myself having a conversation about grief with a stranger on a forest path. But if we are open, aware, and responsive, opportunities to help others will come to us. The chance to help is never very far away.

Such opportunities go hand-in-glove with mediumship. Mediumship is the way we are of service for spirits to effect healing. I recall a particularly challenging time in my life when a message from a medium had the effect of uplifting my own outlook significantly. The prior week had been the anniversary of my husband's death; his birthday was shortly after that. If I threw my late brother's birthday, Father's Day, and my own birthday into the mix, let's just say I could have removed the entire month of June from the calendar without any regrets. But then, there was her message.

"Diane, I felt there was an anniversary of some sort for you," she said. "I am feeling the most 'love you' squeezy hug from a man; like a right 'come here you, I love you' hug. A very intense, passionate hug, I'd say. It was a big 'grab you by the collar to pull you in and throwing arms around you' hug, so much love."

I felt so comforted after this message was delivered to me. Despite growing up knowing the departed are still with me and still love me, the confirmation of that fact never gets old. It continues to comfort me anew every time.

For me, one of the life lessons I learned after David died was that true healing takes place when we understand how we helped ourselves heal, and we share that knowledge with others to help them with their own recovery. It is a bonus if they can also go on to help others. Recognizing the reward of helping others can be a lifesaver for many after they have learned how to save themselves. That was the purpose of my first book, and I think it is the purpose concerning the development of my mediumship too. Yes, a person can go to a medium and receive the healing directly. But when I think back to my early classes in spiritual development, I can see how we can heal ourselves through our efforts.

I recall a session where the point of the exercise was to ask whichever spirit blended with us for a gift. I did, and then I clearly heard the words in my head.

"I gave you the dog."

And I knew David was with me, for he and his dog were inseparable until his death, at which point his brokenhearted dog became mine. And it comforted me to know that he saw me loving his dog as he had. But more importantly, it confirmed again that I could talk to him. I didn't need a third party. I could do this. I could heal myself.

I thought the same thing after the first time I heard music in my head during meditation. It came booming in, and I recognized it as a one-hit wonder by a Swedish rock band from the early seventies.

"Ooga Chaka, Ooga Ooga, Ooga Chaka . . ." It was pounding. I heard it as clearly as if the song were blasting from nearby stereo speakers. I could not seem to *not* hear it. I also had no idea why it was being sent to me. After the session, I looked up the lyrics of the song. It is, in fact, a love song. Once again, I was comforted to know David was still with me. He was talking to me.

Just like my writings had done previously, my meditations taught me that I could self-soothe. I could comfort myself. My book on grief showed me that I could help others heal. Similarly, my entry into the world of mediumship has taught me that I can help others heal by giving healing messages and spiritual healing. I believe my family in the spirit world is pleased. I know they will continue to support me going forward. Meanwhile, I hold them all in my heart with love as I go forward, for I know they hold me in love too. Especially David. For once, a medium gave me a message I hold onto with every fiber of my being.

"The overall feeling I had, which I am sure confirms other readings that you have had, is that your husband is very close to you," he said. "The last thing I remember was seeing you walking towards a sunset horizon with a long (into the distance) veil-like curtain on your right side. I knew he was doing the same on the other side of the curtain, in step!"

It took me a while, but I finally got onto the correct path. It is a path that leads home. It lets me celebrate my family's heritage as I walk in the footsteps of my ancestors. It allows me to embrace my spiritual roots as I learn how to serve Spirit. I am honored to walk among the healers as I travel surrounded by those who love me from the other side of the veil.

EPILOGUE

Once upon a time, in a land far, far away, a boat was being readied to leave the beach. The azure blue water was calm, and the sun shone brightly. The man raised the sail as the vessel was pushed offshore. He had no need for a sextant; he was prepared to rely on the stars. He could see no other shoreline, but he knew where it would be. He set the course in his mind. For he knew she would be waiting.

As the sun dipped from the sky, he moved as one with the water as if willing his connection to it to guide him on his way. As the moon rose in the sky, he sailed on. He was following the moonlight, but he was guided by love. He rested a little but not much, for although he was tired, he was excited to get to his destination. As the pelicans skimmed the small waves at sunrise, he was moved by their graceful "good morning" to him. He basked in the warmth of the sun. He knew this was to be the best day of his life. He could feel it in the depths of his soul. He had been waiting for it for a very long time. As he approached land, he could just make out the figure of a woman. It was her. Just as she had promised, she was finally ready. And she was searching for him.

As the woman caught sight of his approach, she started to run towards the water's edge. He stepped onto the sand to greet her. He was just as she remembered him from all those years ago. They smiled at each other with their eyes. Time stood still as the familiar feelings of love engulfed them. Their hands reached out to one another, and as their fingers touched, they turned into "beings of light" together.

Until then, sweetie, until then.